TRAIL RUNNING

D1178687

Jeff Galloway

Trail Running

Meyer & Meyer Sport

British Library Cataloguing in Publication Data
A catalogue record for this book is available from the British Library

Jeff Galloway: Trail Running
Maidenhead: Meyer & Meyer Sport (UK) Ltd., 2014
ISBN 978-1-78255-011-2

© 2014 by Meyer & Meyer Sport (UK) Ltd.
Aachen, Auckland, Beirut, Budapest, Cairo, Cape Town, Dubai, Hägendorf,
Indianapolis, Maidenhead, Singapore, Sydney, Tehran, Wien
    Member of the World Sport Publishers' Association (WSPA)
    www.w-s-p-a.org
Printed by: B.O.S.S Druck und Medien GmbH, Germany
ISBN 978-1-78255-011-2
E-Mail: info@m-m-sports.com
www.m-m-sports.com

Contents

Chapter 1: Introduction: Trail Running Got Me Hooked on Running

© Jeff Galloway

My first few trail runs did not bring much joy. I was 13, lazy, overweight, and in poor physical shape. Due to my father's Navy career, I had attended 13 schools by the time I finished the 7th grade and had not been involved with team sports or regular physical training of any type. At this point my father became a teacher, we moved to Atlanta, and my new school required each boy to work out with an athletic team after school every day. This was a major jolt to my lazy lifestyle, and I didn't like it.

During the fall I tried football, which was a total disaster from my perspective, and even more so from the view of my coaches. Before choosing a sport for the next quarter, I asked several of the other lazy kids for their choices and was surprised to hear that many had chosen Winter Cross Country Conditioning. The consensus among the slackers was that the coach was the most lenient in the school. "Tell him you are running on the trails, and you only have to jog 200 yards to the woods and hide out."

I did just that for two days. On the third day, an older athlete I liked came over to me and said, Galloway, you're running with us today. I quickly came up with my strategy: As we entered the woods, I planned to grab my hamstring, claiming a muscle pull. But the jokes started right away, and I kept going to hear the punch line. As we entered the trail system, they were exchanging gossip about the teachers—and I wanted to hear all of it. I didn't last long the first day, struggled to adjust to the surface, and walked most of the way back to the school.

The primitive satisfaction of running trails combined with honest friendships and social fun kept me coming back, day after day—but it was hard work. The biggest surprise was how good I felt after a run. The after-run attitude boost was better than I had experienced after any activity during my young life.

There was also something special about the trail experience. Every step was a challenge at first, and I suffered my share of ankle turns and stumbles. With the support of the group, I experienced a unique sense of empowerment from overcoming each challenge.

Week after week I felt my body adapt and improve. The stumbles and aches became fewer and less painful. I began to sense that my feet were making intuitive adjustments to new terrain. I was becoming a trail running animal, and I liked it.

My spirit is energized after every run—but trail running does it better. Touching the earth in a natural environment engages parts of the mind–body network that are not activated on other runs. I felt energized by every trail run during my first few weeks and looked forward to the next one.

The most wonderful aspect of being on the trails after school was the special sense of freedom that can be encountered only on a trail run. When running down the trail, stress melted away: the demanding academic program, conflicts with fellow students, pressure from teachers and parents. As I moved along through the forest and along the creek, I was the king of the trail.

While the causes of stress in my life are different over 50 years later, I enter the same type of enhanced mental restoration today. I love trails!

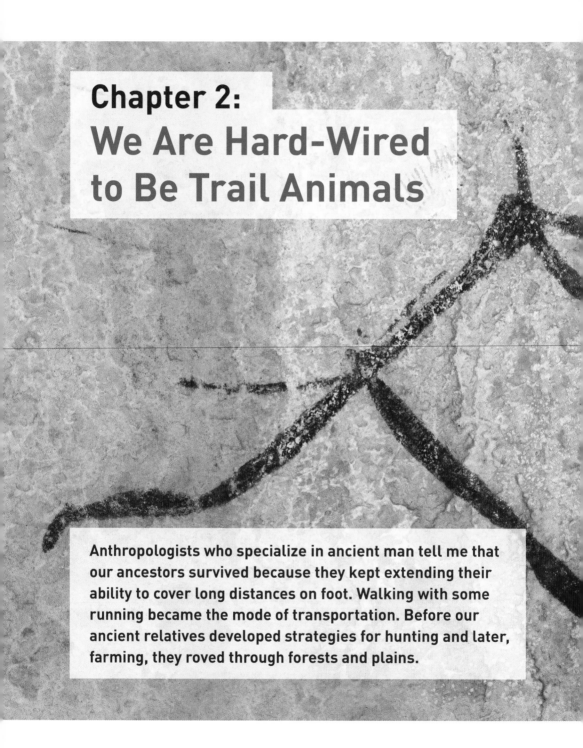

Chapter 2:
We Are Hard-Wired to Be Trail Animals

Anthropologists who specialize in ancient man tell me that our ancestors survived because they kept extending their ability to cover long distances on foot. Walking with some running became the mode of transportation. Before our ancient relatives developed strategies for hunting and later, farming, they roved through forests and plains.

© Thinkstock/iStock

The more ground covered, the greater the chance of finding food. As our forebears pushed back the physical barriers, they developed physiological and mechanical adaptations to keep going…and going…and going.

During the period prior to one million years ago, our ancestors moved from quadruped to biped capabilities and had to solve many problems during the daily journey for food. Trail challenges stimulated brain development in the frontal lobe—the human brain.

Our mind–body organism responds to challenges: When encountering rocks, it is natural to pause, adjust the step, and make little, necessary adjustments. Running requires one to be at a high state of readiness to avoid tripping or stepping in a hole, while maintaining balance and looking ahead to the next challenge.

Scientists have noted that when we're running, thought activity tends to be in the conscious brain, in the frontal lobe. Other animals don't have this "executive brain" resource that allows us humans to be in the moment, to make decisions, and to plan strategically. Neuroscientists believe that during the period of time from 2 million BCE to 1 million BCE, our ancestors expanded their roaming range to find food. As they became endurance animals, they began to band together for survival, developing the human traits of cooperation, trust, and support—while expanding frontal lobe activity.

We return to our roots as we run down the trail.

Chapter 3:
Benefits of
Trail Running

© Thinkstock/iStock

As you move along a trail through forest, desert, or parkland, you enter a different state of mind. You're constantly interacting with the ground, vegetation, elevation change, and a variety of sounds and aromas. Mind–body activity is elevated to a higher level of awareness to be ready to react. You're living in the moment and interacting with life around you as you move forward.

The journey: Our ancestors programmed us to move from one point to another along the trail. Forward movement is positive and fulfilling. Intuitively, as we move forward, we can solve problems and enjoy the satisfaction of exertion in nature. There is a feeling of empowerment in finishing any run, but the sensation has almost always been better at the end of a trail workout.

Sharing: There's a special bonding that occurs when we run with one or more companions along a trail. We're connecting with millions of years of evolution. The extra trust and cooperation felt toward a trail running companion often extends after the run. Some runners communicate and bond better on trails—even when nothing is said. Trail companions are connected the same way our ancient relatives pulled one another along to get through tough times.

Variety: Even if you run the same trail each day, you will feel different sensations on each run. When you choose a different trail every week, you will learn to look forward to the adventure and the discovery process. Each month you can add a few new trails to your favorites. As you get to know different trail connections, you can combine your favorite loops, or out-and-backs to add the distance or time you need on any given day.

The mission: Planning the trail runs usually requires scheduling the drive to and from, assigning time in a busy schedule, coordinating with running companions, and dividing responsibility for logistics. As we work together, anticipate and then experience the trail together, the trail run becomes more than an average run.

Enjoyable scenery: I've run thousands of trail runs. Each has delivered a memorable series of visual images, interesting and diverse sounds, mysteries, and puzzles. Surprising are the discoveries during runs on trails that at first seem boring or not stimulating. Within a few minutes you'll see details of ground cover, vegetation, animal prints or signs, and sounds made by the wind or vegetation. You could write several pages about the details seen and felt along every segment of just about any trail.

Strengthens legs and feet: The legs and feet have to work a bit harder on trails to maintain balance, push off on different terrain, and shift usage of muscles. All of the adaptations for adjusting to various surfaces are embedded in us. As we run regularly on non-paved surfaces, we get better and better at adjusting pace and foot placement, inserting walk breaks, and moving around hazards. You find a different sense of balance on trails. Muscles and tendons intuitively strengthen and work together in special ways during different segments of each trail. You'll notice small muscles not usually defined on road runners are much more defined on the legs of trail runners.

Part of nature: As you move through the trees, plants, hills, grass, and sand, you become part of nature, picking up bits of the forest, field, valley, or prairie. You're literally grounded as you touch earth on each step. You feel the moisture (or lack of) and collect the dust, mist, snow, and frost on you.

Preparation for off-road races: A growing number of races offer off-road races or segments. As you train on trails that simulate your racecourse, you adapt the feet, legs, and balance for the exact demands of the race itself. Many who run trail events will schedule trips to train on the course in advance and reduce the surprises on race day. The best preparation for running on a trail is to train on that trail.

View scenery in a unique way: Due to the light, foliage, and recent precipitation, the scenery changes from one a trail run to any other. Many carry cameras or camera-phones and capture images that are revisited over and over (and often become screen savers), but most of the images are stored away in memory alone. Every week, during a run, a certain image, shadow, or cloud formation will bring flashes of my rich memories in the Sierra Mountains, through Arizona desert preserves, or a Florida longleaf-pine forest. Some were experienced last week but others decades ago—a wonderful and direct connection with our running past.

Brain invigoration: The brain instinctively revs up when you start running on a trail, turning on "circuits" for high awareness. Starting in ancient times, running directly on the earth required more resources throughout the mind–body network. The central nervous system is on high alert, reflexes are ready, and the energy circuit gears up to conserve and deliver as needed. Muscles are activated, performance hormones are released, and mechanical units flow into a smooth range of motion. I know of no other activity that activates our vitality and expectations than trail running.

The result is that I feel more alive and energized when running down a trail: body, mind, and spirit working together. But I'm not alone. Runners tell me every week that they come away from a trail run more energized and motivated than when running on other surfaces.

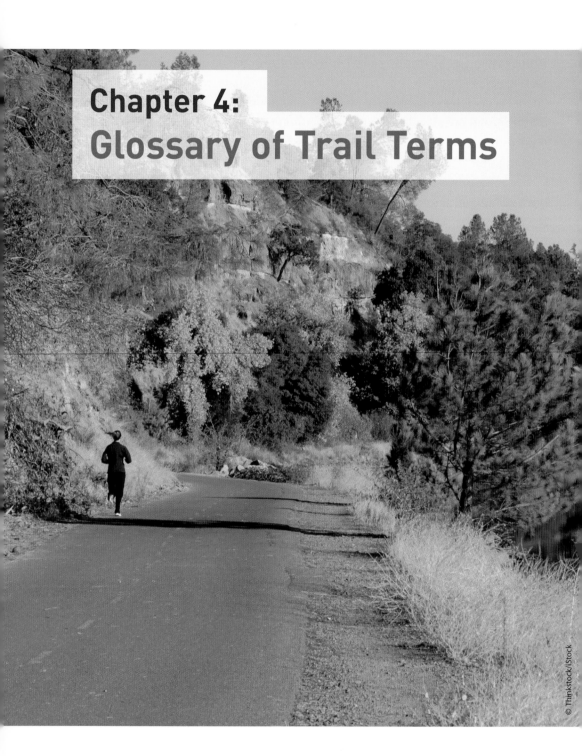

Chapter 4:
Glossary of Trail Terms

Note: Thanks to Kerry Dycus, Chris Twiggs, and Dave James for their input on these issues.

Double track: A two-lane trail such as one made by an ATV or truck. Running side-by-side is possible, passing is easy, and two-way traffic is not a problem. Keep right; pass on the left.

Out-and-back: Running along a trail in one direction for a certain distance, then running back to the start.

Loop trail: A trail that starts and finishes at the same place but has little or no duplication of the route (e.g., making a circle).

Point-to-point: A route that starts in one place and finishes in a different place. Transportation logistics are necessary when setting up such routes.

Single track: This trail is only wide enough for one person at a time. Runners have to yield to other runners to let them pass. Make sure that you leave enough space between you and the runner ahead.

Switchback: A section of trail that makes a zigzag up or down a hill. This is often found when there is a very steep elevation change and is usually preferable to running straight up or down.

Technical: Trails that have lots of rocks, roots, elevation issues, and ditches. Technical trails require a lot more attention than most as foot placement is extremely important. They may also include switchbacks, sharp turns, or blind corners. Technical trails require a delicate balance of looking ahead and looking at the ground in front of you to avoid tripping. As always, take an extra walk break to reduce risks and see what lies ahead.

Trailhead: A location where you can access a trail. Sometimes there is parking and other services. If located in a national or state park, there may be a usage fee. I gladly pay the fee to support upkeep and trail development.

Trail etiquette: This has become an extremely important topic lately as more and more people are taking up trail running: Runners, hikers, cyclists, and sometimes horses will be sharing the same trail. Be aware of the other creatures ahead and behind you.

- **Passing:** When approaching someone who is slower, let them know you are there with a cough or a greeting, such as "How's it going?" Politely thank the yielding runner as you go by after he or she pulls to the side. Uphill runners should yield to downhill runners. The downhill runner has gravity and momentum on his or her side—don't get in the way of either of these. "Passing left" is the best way to let another runner know that you plan to come by, but the person in front needs to be aware that there are faster moving runners behind them as well. For this reason, a lot of trail races forbid headphones.

© Thinkstock/iStock

- **Be patient:** When approaching slower runners on a narrow path, don't put yourself or the other runner at risk. It is appropriate to ask, "Could I please get ahead of you."

- **Being passed:** When running on single track, be aware of those behind who are running faster than you and want to pass. Many single-track races don't have many passing opportunities. When faster runners come up from behind, step aside so that they can pass.

- **Be "green":** Please take your trash with you (gel packs, wrappers, water bottles). Fatigue can result in sloppiness which can lead to litter on the trail.

- **When running with your dog:** Use a leash. A friendly dog can also cause other runners to fall. Always scoop the poop.

- **Stay on the trail:** Obey posted signs and don't cut switchbacks. Some countries do not have the same rules for nature preservation as the United States. If you are competing in a race outside the US, switchback cutting may be allowed, but it's best to stay on the established trail to protect the environment.

- **Buddy system:** The safest trail running, just like the safest road running, is with a buddy. But if you run alone, make sure someone knows your planned route and when to expect you back. Bring your cell phone, ensure there is reception on the trail, and the battery will last for more than the duration of the run.

Chapter 5:
How Do You Find Trails?

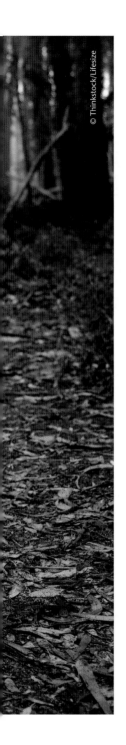

© Thinkstock/Lifesize

Due to the increase in popularity of running and hiking, we're seeing an increase in the number of trails each year. One of the most active organizations is Rails to Trails. This non-profit group buys railroad rights of way and sells it back to local or state governments for local trail development. Visit them at www.railstotrails.org. Many of their projects are finalized with a paved trail but some are not.

A growing number of park departments have websites. When you do a web-search for trails you will often find a website with maps and access points.

Websites to help you find local trails:

www.traillink.com
www.seriousrunning.com
www.trails.com
www.alltrails.com
www.trailrunners.org

Visit the websites for the Appalachian Trail and the Pacific Crest Trail. Both are over 1,000 miles long and have many access points. Some segments will take you into remote areas.

Texastrails.org is an example of the many local organizations that offer directions and a variety of information about the trails in the area. Other examples are Washington Trails Association and www.tejastrails.com (Texas)

A list of trails by state is provided at the end of this book.

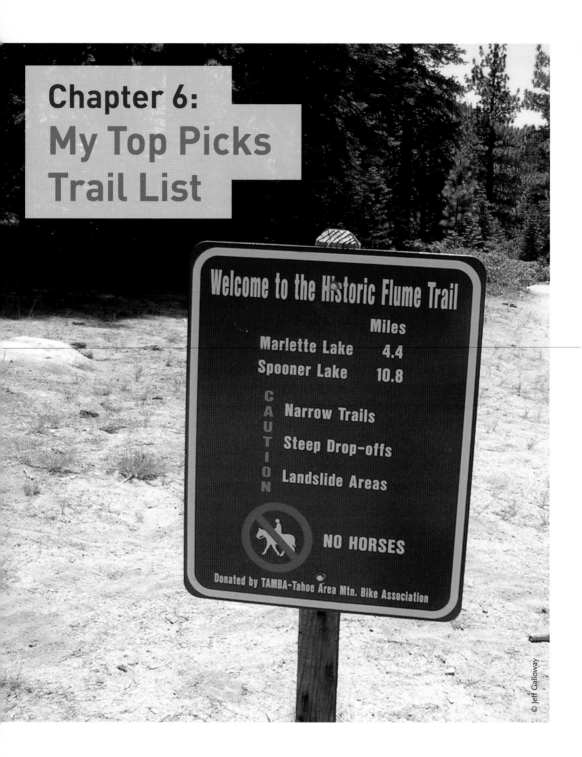

Chapter 6:
My Top Picks
Trail List

Welcome to the Historic Flume Trail

	Miles
Marlette Lake	4.4
Spooner Lake	10.8

CAUTION

Narrow Trails

Steep Drop-offs

Landslide Areas

NO HORSES

Donated by TAMBA-Tahoe Area Mtn. Bike Association

© Jeff Galloway

Tahoe Rim—California/Nevada border

www.tahoerimtrail.org

Every summer, as part of our Tahoe Running Retreat, we hike and run segments of this long trail that runs near the ridgeline of the ancient volcanic crater that forms Lake Tahoe. There are many spectacular segments overlooking the lake. My favorite is on the northeast side in Nevada, just south of the Mount Rose pass on the Mount Rose highway from Incline Village. About half a mile from the summit is a large meadow on the east side of the road. At the south end of this meadow is a trailhead. Within a mile and a half you will move from meadow, to pine forest, to hillside, and even desert landscapes. Then you can enjoy a continuing series of magnificent views of Lake Tahoe. You can go as far as you wish, then turn around. Most of the trail surface is stable with visible logs and rocks.

The Tahoe Flume Trail

Not far from the trail listed above is the Flume Trail. The trailhead is just south of Incline Village, Nevada, at the northeast end of Lake Tahoe. It takes about an hour to hike the three miles to the Flume Trail after about 1,000 feet of elevation gain. During the gold-rush days this was a water flume to move logs along the mountain toward Virginia City's mines. The elevation change once on the flume is minimal and the views are spectacular. This can be an out-and-back or a point-to-point leading to Spooner Summit trailhead.

The Perimeter Trail—
Ouray Colorado

www.ouraytrails.org/trails09.html

The Perimeter Trail around Ouray, Colorado is amazing. Within the first half-mile, runners are treated to an amazing view of an incredible waterfall. As the name suggests, the Perimeter Trail follows a route around the circumference of Ouray, while seemingly travelling back in time. You'll see remnants of an old mine passing through a mining tunnel that hovers above the Box Canyon. Portions of this trail are used in the annual Hardrock Hundred Mile Endurance Run, one of the toughest footraces on Earth. Nonetheless, the Perimeter Trail is accessible for runners of all skill levels, as well as day-hikers, and is a must for anyone visiting the San Juan region of southwest Colorado. The photo taken from the Perimeter Trail will look familiar to fans of John Wayne's movie *True Grit*, which is not to be confused with the remake. This same view appears during the famous snake pit scene in that film.

Blue Mountain Beach Trails—In the Florida Panhandle
between Destin and Panama City

www.floridaforestservice.com/state_forests/sf_pdf/pt_washington_trails.pdf

This is the location of our Galloway Beach Retreats. After a two-minute jog along a bike trail, you enter Point Washington State Forest, which is connected to Grayton Beach State Park. This area is full of trails and loops through longleaf-pine forests and cypress trees, with good and stable footing in almost all areas.

The previous link shows only the main trail, but there are hundreds of loops and extensions throughout. In addition, the beautiful white sand beach and several other parks nearby offer a wonderland of views, sunsets, sunrises, wildlife, nature, and peaceful runs.

Pre's Trail—Eugene, Oregon, Memorial to Steve Prefontaine

www.eugene-or.gov/index.aspx?NID = 1727]

I visited Eugene, Oregon many times the late 60s and early 70s when there were very few trails with stable footing. There I met Bill Bowerman, who was in charge of my Munich Olympic team. Bill was one of the leading forces in running during that era, an innovator, and a major influence on my running life.

He promoted a few runs a week on trails, especially wood chips and shredded tires to strengthen feet and legs. One of Bill's athletes and my best friend, Geoff Hollister (see Hollister Trail next), introduced me to another Oregon distance runner, Steve Prefontaine (see the movie *Prefontaine*), who also became a close friend. During our warm-up before workouts and on long runs, Pre and I explored some trails on the north side of the Willamette River from the university of Oregon campus. At the time the surface was not ideal but added a few miles and some variety to our runs. After Pre's untimely death in 1975, the Eugene community developed a wood chip and asphalt trail system in the same area where we ran and named it after their inspiring athlete. It's accessible from the campus and several other areas.

Geoff Hollister Trail—Near the Nike Campus in Beaverton, Oregon

More than any other person, my friend Geoff Hollister, as the promotions director for Nike during the early years, helped make running part of the American lifestyle. His book *Out of Nowhere* is filled with stories of the first great running boom in the 70s and early 80s. Nike has commemorated his efforts by establishing and naming a fitness trail in Geoff's honor adjacent to the Nike campus in Beaverton, Oregon.

Western States Trail—Squaw Valley, California, Rim Trail

The Western States Trail was used by immigrants before roads were established between the Lake Tahoe area and Auburn and Sacramento in California. The Western States 100-mile trail race is the unofficial 100-mile world championship, starting in Squaw Valley (where our summer running retreat takes place) and finishing in Auburn, California. It is generally on the rugged side with many segments of rocks and ruts, so you will have to watch your footing. You should also get a trail map from one of the outdoor stores in the area because there are lots of trail intersections. My favorite segment of this trail can either be a point-to-point or out-and-back. It starts along the Truckee River between Squaw Valley and Alpine Meadows at the north end of the highway 89 bridge over the river. It leads across a few small creeks, through meadows, up to the Ridgeline between Squaw Valley and Alpine Meadows with a wonderful view above Squaw Valley. Taking a dirt road down about half a mile, you can then connect with a single track trail that offers a series of great vistas of Squaw Valley, about 600 feet below. This connects with a dirt road for the last three-quarter mile down to the Squaw Valley Lodge—the home of our summer retreat.

Walden Pond Trail—Near Lincoln, Massachusetts, made famous by Thoreau and Bill Rodgers

Bill won both the New York Marathon and the Boston Marathon—four times each. Before those accomplishments, Bill and I were teammates at Wesleyan University. He has always loved running on trails, feeling that his early trail running developed strength in feet and ankles, which carried over into his road running.

Bill told me about this trail, and I love it. While running around Walden Pond, you understand why the philosopher Henry David Thoreau was attracted to the area. This is truly a transcendental run. Bill also likes the Assabet Park in Maynard and Marlboro, Massachusetts.

Note: Be sure to look at the last section of this book for a listing of trails by state.

Chapter 7:
Shoes—Choosing the Best Shoe for You

The best advice I can give you about trail shoes is to get the best advice. If you have a good technical running store in your area, go there and ask for the staff person who is the most knowledgeable in fitting trail shoes. The advice you can receive from experienced shoe fitters is priceless. The better stores conduct on-going training with all staff members so they know the following:

1. How to identify how each person's two feet naturally move when they walk and when they run.
2. Which shoes are designed for the function of each foot.
3. Which shoes in a function category are best for various foot shapes and sizes.
4. Which shoes offer protection and solve problems in various situations.
5. What are the technical aspects of trail shoes—for terrain, surface, and protection.

Well-trained staff members will work with you to find several possibilities. They are your consultants who can identify possible problems and suggest specific shoes as you walk and run in various shoes, describing how each feels on your feet.

Top priority: Find a basic training shoe that will support your foot. Most runners will do most of their running on paved surfaces and will need a shoe with sufficient cushion that allows the foot to function in its natural way. Go through the fitting process for an everyday shoe first.

Trail shoes? There are many good trail shoes, which are designed for various types of terrain. Many runners, however, can use their everyday shoes on trails. Before investing in a trail shoe, it's best to try running in your regular pair on a short trail. Most of the trails I run don't require a trail shoe. This "trial trail run" will identify possible problems that you can talk over with your shoe-fitting expert.

- **Protection for the foot:** If a significant portion of your miles are run on rocks or gravel, there are many trail shoes that can protect the foot.
- **Toe protection:** If you experience toe impact from very rocky trails, look at a shoe with a toe guard.
- **Loose dirt or sand:** Shoes that have knobs, waffles, or other projections from the sole can give better traction.
- **Motion control shoes:** On uneven terrain, these shoes can be too stiff and cause injuries.
- **Gore-Tex:** Waterproof cloth will often increase sweating and heat build-up. When running through streams, water usually enters the shoe over the ankle and is trapped in shoes that are waterproof.

No expert in the area? If you don't have a really experienced shoe advisor in your area, try this do-it-yourself plan:

1. Look at the wear pattern on your most worn pair of walking or running shoes. Use the following guide to help you choose about three pairs of shoes from one of the categories:

Can't tell?
Choose shoes that are neutral or mid range of cushion and support.

- Set aside at least 30 minutes to choose your next shoe.
- Run and walk, on a pavement surface, to compare the shoes. If you have a floppy foot, make sure that you get the support you need.
- You want a shoe that feels natural on your foot—no pressure or aggravation—while allowing the foot to go through the range of motion needed for running.
- Again, take as much time as you need before deciding.
- If the store doesn't let you run in the shoe, go to another store.

Heel wear is usually not as important as forefoot wear. Most runners hit first on the outside of the heel and experience more wear in this area. If you have a wear pattern on the inside of the heel and are experiencing pain in the knee, hip, or ankle, you should try shoes that are not too soft or wobbly on your feet.

Floppy feet have spots of wear, including some wear on the inside of the forefoot.

If your shoes show this pattern, and you are experiencing some foot or knee pain, select a shoe that has minimal cushion, is not too high off the ground and is not too soft.

Overpronated foot: This floppy foot pattern shows significant wear on the inside of the forefoot. If there is knee or hip pain, look for a shoe that has more stability. If you don't have pain, look at a neutral shoe that does not have a lot of cushion in the forefoot—or choose a shoe that is similar to one that is working for you currently.

Note: Don't try to fix a foot that is not broken. Just because you roll excessively to the inside does not mean you should choose a motion control shoe. If you have no foot, knee, or hip problems and are using a neutral or even fairly cushioned shoe with success, stay with the type of shoe that is working for you.

Rigid: If you have a wear pattern on the outside and middle of the forefoot of the shoe and no wear on the inside, you have a rigid foot and can choose a neutral shoe that has adequate cushion and flexibility for you as you run and walk in them.

Can't tell: Start with several neutral shoes, or shoes that are very similar to those that have worked for you before. Walk and then run in several models. If your foot does not feel supported or is not working in a natural way, try a different shoe.

1. Set aside at least 30 minutes to choose your next shoe so that you can compare the three final candidates you have chosen.
2. Run and walk, on a pavement surface, to compare the shoes. If you have a floppy or over-pronated foot, make sure that you get the support you need. Often the signs of minimal support are irritation of weak links in the hip, knee, or foot when using one shoe and not with another model.
3. You want a shoe that feels natural—no pressure or irritation—while allowing the foot to go through your natural range of motion when running and walking. Runners that need motion control should feel reasonably secure in the shoe.
4. Take as much time as you need before deciding.
5. If the store doesn't let you run in the shoe, go to another store.

Does the size seem too big? Don't worry about the size on the box—go for the fit. Most runners wear a running shoe that is about one-half to two sizes larger than their street shoe. For example, I wear a size 10 street shoe but run in a size 12 running model.

There should be room in the toe region. Leave about half to three-quarters of an inch of extra toe room. Your foot tends to swell during the day, so it's best to fit your shoes in the afternoon. Be sure to stand up in the shoe during the fitting process to measure how much extra room you have in the toe region of the shoe. Pay attention to the longest of your feet, and leave at least half an inch.

Width issues:

- Running shoes tend to be a bit wider than street shoes—but a few models come in widths.
- Usually, the lacing can "snug up" the difference, if your foot is a bit narrower.
- The shoe shouldn't be laced too tight around your foot because the foot swells during running and walking. On hot days, the average runner will move up a half shoe size.
- In general, running shoes are designed to handle a certain amount of "looseness," but if you are getting blisters when wearing a loose shoe, tighten the laces.
- Some shoe companies have some models that come in widths.
- The shoe is too narrow if you are rolling off the edge of the shoe as you push off—on either side.

© Thinkstock/iStock

Shoes for women:

Women's shoes tend to be slightly narrower than those for men, and the heel is usually a bit smaller. About 25% of women runners have feet that can fit better into men's shoes—usually in the larger sizes. The better running stores can help you make a choice in this area.

Choosing trail shoes:

The first part of the trail shoe fitting process should be the same as for an everyday running shoe. Once you determine the pattern of movement and support needs, you can move on to choosing a trail shoe.

Minimal support shoes:

About every 10 years, a new wave of minimal shoes returns to the market. These feel good when running on carpet, golf courses, or beaches. Without protection, however, they don't protect the foot from rocks, sharp objects, uneven terrain, and the pounding of pavement. I've heard from thousands who have been injured when wearing these and I don't recommend them for everyday use or on trails.

Breaking in a new shoe:

- Wear the new shoe around the house, for an hour or more each day for a week. If you stay on carpet and the shoe doesn't fit correctly, you can exchange it at the store, but if you have put some wear and dirt on the shoe, few stores will take it back.
- In most cases, runners find that shoes are comfortable enough to run immediately. It is best, however, to continue walking in the shoe, gradually allowing the foot to accommodate to the arch, the heel, the ankle pads, and to make other adjustments. If you run in the shoe too soon, blisters are often the result.
- If there are no rubbing issues on the foot when walking, you could walk in the new shoe for a gradually increasing amount, for two to four days.
- At that point, run about half a mile in the shoe. Then put on your old shoes and continue the run.
- On each successive run, increase the distance run in the new shoe for three to four runs. At this point, you will usually have the new shoe broken in.

© Thinkstock/iStock

How do you know when it's time to get a new shoe?

- When you have been using a shoe for three to four weeks successfully, buy another pair of exactly the same model, make, and size. The reason for this: The shoe companies often make significant changes or discontinue shoe models (even successful ones) every six to eight months.
- Walk around the house in the new shoe for a few days.
- After the shoe feels broken in, run the first or last half mile of one of your weekly runs (shoe break-in day) in the new shoe, then put on the shoe that is already broken in.
- On this weekly shoe comparison, gradually run a little more in the new shoe.
- Several weeks later you will notice that the new shoe offers more bounce than the old one.
- When the old shoe doesn't offer the support you need, shift to the new pair.
- Start breaking in a third pair.

Socks

The sock market has exploded in the last 10 years. There are many variables to consider, which makes your choice more difficult at first but increases your chance of getting socks that fit your feet and pattern of running. Be sure you try on a new pair of shoes using the type of sock you will be wearing.

- Don't wear cotton! Moisture will be absorbed and will stay in the sock, increasing the weight of the shoes and the chance of blisters.

- Thick or thin—this is usually a personal preference. Thick socks offer more protection but may bunch up. They may also retain more moisture.

- Low or high cut—some runners will wear two layers: a higher sock or compression sleeve over the calf for protection from weeds, poison ivy, or

poison oak. The lower profile sock will give an extra layer of support to the foot. Be sure to try on shoes with both layers.

- Micro fiber—there are many socks of high-tech fibers that will move the moisture away from the foot for better comfort. This is particularly important when running through puddles or streams during trail runs.

- Compression—research shows many benefits from wearing compression garments on the calf muscle: better blood circulation, quicker recovery, and even faster times in races. Some runners like to have a one-piece compression sock that goes over the calf. Others prefer to have a compression sleeve from the ankle to the calf and then a compression, or other sock, on the foot.

© Thinkstock/iStock

Chapter 8:
Clothing

Weather issues: Adverse weather creates more challenges in trail areas, and it's best to be prepared for any reasonable weather change. When running in cities or suburbs, one can seek refuge in a store or house, for example. If it starts sleeting or snowing when you are five miles into the woods, though, you'll have to rely upon what you have with you.

Obviously you don't have to be prepared for a snow storm during a summer run in Texas, so check the weather forecast and radar before venturing into the woods, and you will have a good idea about what to bring.

Many trail runners have a backpack with garments for every type of weather condition. They'll look through the bag and take only the items that are most likely to be needed during the hours projected for the run and afterward, before leaving the car or house.

Protection from briars, poison ivy, poison oak, or other plants: Clothing can protect you from the bushes and weeds that line the trail. On many summer runs, you'll find that vegetation can grow across the trail, forcing you to walk or run through. Since you don't want to wear too much during the hot months, compression sleeves or leggings can protect without increasing your body temperature significantly.

Layers for cold temperatures: The Clothing Thermometer following this section has recommendations for various temperatures. As the temperature drops, put on the extra layers. A good high-tech fiber on the skin can maintain body temperature while releasing extra heat. These fibers also transport moisture away from the skin so that it can be evaporated on the outside layer. It helps to have a long-sleeved garment as the outer layer. If you warm up during the run, you can peel it off and tie it around your waist. If you cool off later, put it back on.

© Thinkstock/Fuse

39

The clothing thermometer

After years of coaching runners in various climates, here are my recommendations for the appropriate clothing based upon the temperature. The first layer, since it will be on your skin, should feel comfortable and designed to move the moisture away from your skin. You may have to resist the temptation to buy a fashionable color, because function is most important. As you try on the clothing in the store, watch for seams and extra material in areas where you will have body parts rubbing together thousands of times during a run.

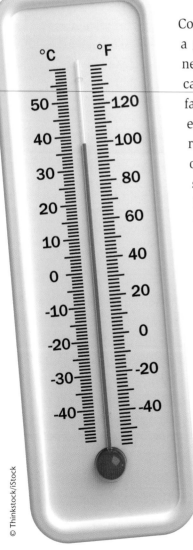

Cotton is usually not a good fabric for those who perspire a great deal. The cotton will absorb the sweat, hold it next to your skin, and increase the weight you must carry during the run. Garments made out of high-tech fabric, such as Polypro, Coolmax, and Drifit, can retain enough body heat to keep you warm in winter, while releasing the extra amount. Moving moisture to the outside of the garment will allow you to stay cooler in summer, while avoiding the winter chill. A new fabric by Mizuno, called Breaththermo, actually heats up with modest perspiration in the winter.

Temperature	What to wear
14 °C or 60 °F and above	Tank top, or singlet, and shorts
9 to 13 °C or 50 to 59 °F	T-shirt and shorts
5 to 8 °C or 40 to 49 °F	Long-sleeve, light-weight shirt, shorts or tights (or nylon long pants), mittens and gloves
0 to 4 °C or 30 to 39 °F	Long-sleeve, medium-weight shirt and another t-shirt, tights and shorts, socks, mittens or gloves, and a hat over the ears
-4 to -1 °C or 20 to 29 °F	Medium-weight, long-sleeve shirt, another t-shirt, tights and shorts, socks, mittens or gloves, and a hat over the ears
-8 to -3 °C or 10 to 19 °F	Medium-weight, long-sleeve shirt, and medium- to heavy-weight shirt, tights and shorts, nylon wind suit, top and pants, socks, thick mittens, and a hat over the ears
-12 to -7 °C or 0 to 9 °F	Two medium- or heavy-weight long-sleeve tops, thick tights, thick underwear (especially for men), medium to heavy warm up, gloves and thick mittens, ski mask, a hat over the ears, and Vaseline covering any exposed skin
-18 to -11 °C or -15 °F	Two heavy-weight, long-sleeve tops, tights and thick tights, thick underwear (and supporter for men), thick warm-up (top and pants), mittens over gloves, thick ski mask and a hat over ears, Vaseline covering any exposed skin, thicker socks on your feet, and other foot protection, as needed
Minus 20° both C & F	Add layers as needed

What not to wear

- A heavy coat in winter. If the layer is too thick, you'll heat up, sweat excessively, and cool too much when you take it off.
- No shirt for men in summer. Fabric that holds some of the moisture will give you more of a cooling effect as you run and walk.
- Too much sun screen—it can interfere with sweating.
- Too thick socks in summer. Your feet swell, and the pressure from the socks can increase the chance of a black toenail and blisters.
- Lime green shirt with bright pink polka dots (unless you have a lot of confidence or need visibility when hunters are in the area).

© Thinkstock/iStock

Special cases:

Chaffing can be reduced by Lycra and other fabric. Many runners have eliminated chaffing between the legs by using a Lycra "bike tight" as an undergarment. These are also called *Lycra shorts*. There are also several skin lubricants on the market, including the products by the company 2Toms.

Some men suffer from irritation of their nipples. Having a slick and smooth fabric across the chest will reduce this. There is now a product called Nip-Guard that has reduced the chance of having this problem.

Do your running clothes smell? There is an excellent detergent from 2Toms that goes into the fibers and attacks and eliminates the causes of odor.

Chapter 9: Caution! Rough Road Ahead—The Unique Challenges

© Jeff Galloway

Rules of the trail

- **Run with a buddy or two**

- **Bring a cell phone**

- **Research the area for risks—and avoid them**

- **Wear adequate clothing**

- **Walk gently through hazards**

Who should not run trails: Those of us who love running on trails want all of our friends to enjoy it. Unfortunately, some will be miserable or will suffer repeat injuries when running in the natural environment. Through gradually introducing the feet, legs, and psyche to trail running, there is a chance that even those who hated trails at first will become trail lovers. Everyone needs to be careful in the beginning, though.

Weak ankles put one at risk on uneven terrain. Those with very mobile ankle joints are very likely to suffer ankle sprains, strains, and tendon irritation in other areas. I've run with some weak ankle runners and just about any irregularity can set off the movement that can cause irritation and injury.

Foot, knee, and hip issues can be triggered by uneven terrain. More walking and strengthening exercises can reduce the risk, but those who have repeat injuries in these areas when they take to the trails should look to a pedestrian or bike trail system with a paved surface.

Some runners are anxious when they run away from "civilization." The fear of the unknown is real and will leave anxious runners with a negative feeling after a trail run. Gradually venturing into woods or parks can sometimes allow runners to adapt and de-sensitize to the emotions. Running with the right companion(s) can also help deal with this.

If you are running with someone who is challenged by any of these issues, talk about the problems and the solutions. This focuses mental activity into the conscious brain—which can give one control over the subconscious, emotional brain.

Buddy system: Always go with another person. Accidents happen to the most experienced trail runners, and no one is exempt from unexpected adverse weather. Those who run alone are putting themselves at risk in several threatening areas: wildlife, getting lost, or medical emergencies.

Shoes: Do some research on the trail you will be running. This will help you choose which shoe to wear. Many trails allow for regular running shoes. Those who have unstable ankles should wear shoes that are lower to the ground when running on trails. When there is gravel or sharp objects, trail shoes with foot protection will help. Ask some veteran trail runners who have used the trail you will be running—or shoe store staff who are very knowledgeable about trail shoes.

Look ahead and walk when needed. While running, we often rely on momentum to maintain balance. This can get us into trouble when we try to run through a trail segment with lots of debris. Keep looking ahead on the trail for possible surface hazards. Always err on the safe side by walking gently to maintain control.

Getting lost? Some runners don't have a good sense of direction. When running in a group of two or more, make sure that one member knows the trail really well or has an excellent sense of direction. Just to be sure, bring some bright-colored plastic flagging ribbon (sometimes called surveyor's tape) and mark the trail at regular intervals. The ribbons will be very helpful when you are returning through an intersection of trails. As you move away from each ribbon, look back and visualize what you will see when returning.

Carry a cell phone—with reception. Every year a number of runners and hikers are saved because they brought their cell phone. Make sure that the phone can be used in the area you are running.

—just in case. Those who run in the early morning or at dusk tend to bring flashlights. It only takes one wrong turn, and you could be in the wilderness when the sun goes down.

Trail safety:

Each year I hear about the accidents experienced by dozens of trail runners. Most of these are preventable. Here are the primary causes, and what you can do about them:

- **You are not focusing on the surface.**
  Always be on guard—even when the trail seems to be smooth and comfortable. Be aware of anything that could cause a fall and avoid it. If there are a series of surface challenges, walk slowly or stop and set up a plan for getting through the areas.

  Be aware of your surroundings. I know it is wonderful to be on "cruise control" in your right brain, but you need to be aware of the path ahead to avoid a dangerous fall. Just keep looking around and anticipate.

  When running or walking with another person, don't try to follow blindly on the trail. Allow for 10 to 15 paces or so between you and the runner ahead. This allows you to see the surface and take action. Runners who pick up the pace around a curve can be surprised when they round the corner. Be cautious. Look at the side of the trail and have an option for diversion if the surface is slippery or there are unexpected obstacles.

- **Sometimes runners get distracted by conversations and scenery.**
  One of the very positive aspects of running becomes a negative one in this case. Yes, do chat and enjoy time with your friends. But every runner in a group needs to be responsible for his or her own safety and footing. Runners at the back of a group should never assume that they don't have to be concerned about hazards at all. Be responsible for your own safety.

- **In general, be ready to save yourself from a variety of trail problems by following the rules listed. Even if the rules seem obvious, many runners incur serious injuries on trails.**

- Be aware of the health and fitness ability of your running companions. You don't want someone to get into a challenge that could leave them without energy or muscle power to run out of the forest.

- Go over the trail map regularly and check the map. Make notes so that you can re-trace your steps if you get lost. Think ahead at all times with a plan for any challenge.

- Bring lights on all afternoon runs. Some runners get lost on trails and have to find their way back in the dark.

- Take control over your safety—you are the only one on the trail who will usually save yourself.

© Thinkstock/iStock

Chapter 10:
Equipment

© Thinkstock/iStock

To prepare for various challenges along the trail, you'll need supplies. Listed in this chapter are the key items used by trail runners. As you gain more experience, you may add individual items.

Make a list and check it twice. Keep a running list of items, with your belt or pack, so that you can do an inventory before each run. When you return, replace items used and add to the list when you find another item that would be helpful.

You don't need all of these items on every run. On short trail runs, where you know your way, you may not need any of them. When in doubt, bring it!

Trail checklist

Supply/hydration belt: I like the products under the Fitletic by iFitness brand: belts, hydration carriers, and pouches. These are the best belts I've seen and used for staying snug around the waist. I love the bib holder, which eliminates pinning bib numbers on shirts in races. The company keeps innovating to improve in various ways. The newest version allows for two

16- to 20-ounce bottles and flaps to hold gel packs and other items. The central pouch has room for most cell phones as well as storage for hotel keys or car keys. The arm pouch (which wraps around the biceps) and hand carriers have also been popular.

When you need more water: For very long runs, where water is not available, the camelback products are popular. The large bladder of water is carried like a backpack, and you can use a tube to suck the water you need.

© Thinkstock/Digital Vision

- **Backpack:** To comfortably carry what you need. There are many different versions at running stores and outdoor stores.
- **Cellphone:** Make sure it is charged.
- **GPS:** For when the area is confusing, when exploring a new trail, or if you get lost.
- **Map of area:** If there are many intersections of trails, a map of the area can be invaluable.
- **Flashlight:** If you might be running in the dark or at dusk.
- **Flagging:** To mark the right trail at an intersection on your return.
- **Water:** Especially on runs longer than 90 minutes.
- **Snacks:** Especially on runs longer than 90 minutes.
- **Pepper spray:** If you suspect that wild animals could be in the area.
- **First aid kit:** Band aids, Neosporin, antiseptic wipes, individual items.
- **Bug spray:** If there are mosquitoes, stinging flies, or other bugs that bite.
- **Sunscreen:** Towelettes or wipes.
- **Poison ivy and poison oak prevention and treatment.**
- **Garbage bags:** In case of rain. Cut out a hole for the head.
- **Gaiters:** To keep debris out of your shoes.
- **Compression sleeves:** For faster recovery and protection from poison ivy, poison oak, briars, and other vegetation.
- **Technical equipment for special trails:** Individual needs should be addressed.
- **Gripping gloves and shoes:** Chosen as needed.

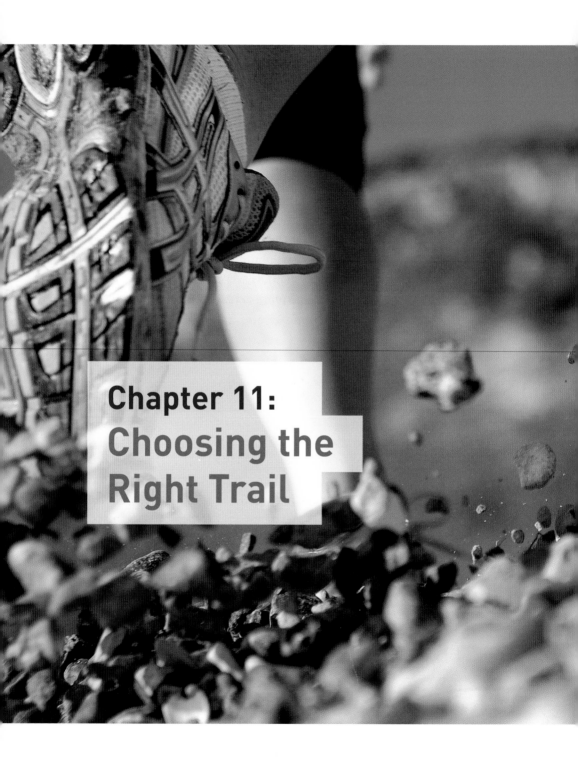

Chapter 11: Choosing the Right Trail

© Thinkstock/iStock

Trails vary greatly in difficulty. Some are flat, gentle, without confusing cross trails. Other trail systems are full of rocks, roots, erosion, and other hazards. It pays to do your trail homework.

Some trails become a lot more difficult during and after a rainstorm. Ask whether certain areas are prone to flash floods, quicksand, mudslides, or rock slides.

Consult local trail runners. Through your local running store or running club you can probably connect with local trail runners. Tell the expert the type of trail you would like to run, as well as hazards you'd like to avoid.

Find a map! Some running and outdoor stores have trail maps. You may also find these at the local office of your state or U.S. Forest Service, or state or National Park office. The websites of many state and National parks will often have trail maps.

Be aware of animal threats. Ask if there have been sightings of aggressive animals such as bears, mountain lions, wild hogs, or wild dogs. In wilderness areas, moose and even deer have been known to run over humans, resulting in significant injury and death.

Are there poisonous snakes, spiders, or other threats? If so, find out where they have been seen, how to avoid contact, and what time of the day is best to avoid them.

Know if there are disease-carrying insects that can carry lime disease or West Nile virus. The local health department usually tracks cases of such afflictions and where they were acquired.

Are you allergic to any plants or shrubs in the area? If so, cover yourself and reduce the possible skin contact. Carry medication in case you need it—to reduce the downtime. If you have problems with poison ivy or poison oak, look up pictures of leaf shape and structure and be vigilant. Cover exposed skin.

Make sure the trail area is safe. Most local trail runners can tell you about safety issues that are not covered above. Ask if cars have been broken into at the trailhead—or if other crime has been observed in the area.

Trail challenges

After talking to trail runners, mark possible challenges on your trail map. Before beginning your trail run, note the hazardous places. If there are a continuing series of hazards, break out the map every 10-15 minutes and look at the next trail segment.

Prevention is the best strategy to avoid ankle sprains or other injuries. Walk carefully through uneven areas, and you can reduce your risk.

- Rocks: Shoes only help to a certain point. When the surface is too unstable, you need to walk carefully.
- Roots: It is easy to trip when there are a lot of roots in the area. It's best to walk and stay focused on each root ahead.
- Ruts: Erosion can change a smooth trail into a very rugged one in an hour or two.
- Hidden risks: During fall and winter, leaves can cover potholes, rocks, and other trail obstacles. Walk through potentially hazardous areas.
- Steep downhill: It is common to slip on dirt, leaves, sand, rocks, or slick rock faces when running downhill. Manage your pace by slowing down or walking before you get out of control.
- Flash floods: Note the low places on your map and work out a strategy to escape if it starts raining. If your map has contour lines, you can find higher ground.
- Slippery surface: With water present, your footing can be unexpectedly slippery. Situations that should trigger careful footing include the following: near creeks and rock faces that have drainage during or after a rain (even a light rain).
- Lightning: During a lightning storm, it's best to take cover—and avoid higher elevations.
- Where do runners tend to get lost? Most experienced trail runners can tell you. Mark your maps and then use flagging tape to mark the correct trail. Even the correct path looks different on the way back.

Chapter 12:
The Galloway
Run-Walk-Run
Method

© Thinkstock/Comstock

**Run strong to the end ...
Better control on uneven terrain**

The correct Run-Walk-Run strategy on trail runs allows you to be more resilient at the end of tiring runs, with less fatigue. You can carry on your life activities after long runs.

Walk before you get tired.

Most of us, even when untrained, can walk for several miles before fatigue sets in, because walking is an activity that we can do efficiently for hours. Running is more work, because you have to lift your body off the ground and then absorb the shock of the landing, over and over. The continuous use of the running muscles will produce more fatigue, aches, and pains than maintaining the same pace while taking walk breaks. If you walk before your running muscles start to get tired, you allow the muscle to recover instantly—increasing your capacity for exercise while reducing the chance of next-day soreness.

The "method" part involves having a strategy. By using a ratio of running and walking that is right for you on each day, you can manage your fatigue. You are the one who is strong to the finish, doing what you need or want to do after long runs. You never have to be exhausted after a long run again.

The run-walk method is very simple: You run for a short segment and then take a walk break, and keep repeating this pattern.

Walk breaks:

- Allow you to have more control when running on rocky, rooty, or slippery trails.

- Give you control over the way you feel at the end.

- Erase fatigue—walk break by walk break.

- Push back your fatigue wall.

- Allow for endorphins to collect during each walk break—you feel good!

- Break up the distance into manageable units ("two more minutes" or "thirty more seconds").

- Speed recovery.

- Reduce the chance of aches, pains, and injury.

- Allow you to feel good afterward—carrying on the rest of your day without debilitating fatigue.

- Give you all of the endurance of the distance of each session—without the pain.

- Allow older runners or heavier runners to recover fast and feel as good or better as the younger (slimmer) days.

- Activate the frontal lobe, keeping you in control over your attitude and motivation.

Use a short and gentle walking stride

It's better to walk slowly, with a short stride. There has been some irritation of the shins when runners or walkers maintain a stride that is too long. Relax and enjoy the walk.

Don't eliminate the walk breaks

Some beginners assume that they must work toward the day when they don't have to take any walk breaks at all. This is up to the individual, but is not recommended—especially when running trails. Remember that you decide what ratio of Run-Walk-Run to use. There is no rule that requires you to hold to any ratio on a given day. As you adjust the run-walk to how you feel, you gain control over your fatigue.

Adjust walk break amounts and frequency on trails

Because of terrain and moisture issues, trail runners must be ready to take more frequent walk breaks to gain control over balance. By slowing down and walking at the first sign of debris ahead, you can assess the situation, adjust your stride, and maintain control.

The best way to deal with weak ankles, feet, and knees is to prevent problems by walking before you step on something that turns your feet. On rough trails, you will be taking more walk breaks.

Falls are a common cause of injury. Runners who try to run through a debris field are more likely to fall on the rocks or roots that caused the fall.

Walk up hills

It is common practice among trail runners, in races or training runs, to walk most or all of the hills. Those who have compared their times—walking up a trail hill and then running up the same hill—have found that the time was not significantly different, but the fatigue was a lot greater when running uphill. I've run for over 50 years, and one of the extra running "freedoms" on trails is taking walk breaks when you want or need to do so. I enjoy running on trails more than ever because of walk breaks.

How to keep track of the walk breaks

On smooth trails, you can use a timer that tells you when to run and then when to walk. The best product is the Galloway Run-Walk-Run timer, which will beep or vibrate. There are several watches that can be set for two intervals. Check our website: www.jeffgalloway.com.

Run-Walk-Run ratios on smooth trails

After having heard back from over 300,000 runners who have used walk breaks at various paces, I've come up with the following suggested ratios:

Pace per mile	Run amount	Walk amount
7:00	6 minutes	30 seconds (or run a mile/walk 40 seconds)
7:30	5 minutes	30 seconds
8:00	4 minutes	30 seconds
8:30	4 minutes	45 seconds
9:00	4 minutes	1 minute
9:30	3 minutes	45 seconds
10:00-10:45	3 minutes	1 minute
10:45-11:45	2:30 minutes	1 minute
11:45-12:45	2 minutes	1 minute
12:45-13:30	1 minute	1 minute
13:30-14:30	30 seconds	30 seconds
14:30-15:30	20 seconds	40 seconds
15:30-17:00	15 seconds	45 seconds
17:00-18:30	10 seconds	50 seconds
18:30-20:00	5 seconds	55 seconds

Note: You may always divide each of the amounts by two. Example: Instead of running 12-min/mi pace using 2-1, you could run for 1 minute and walk for 30 seconds.

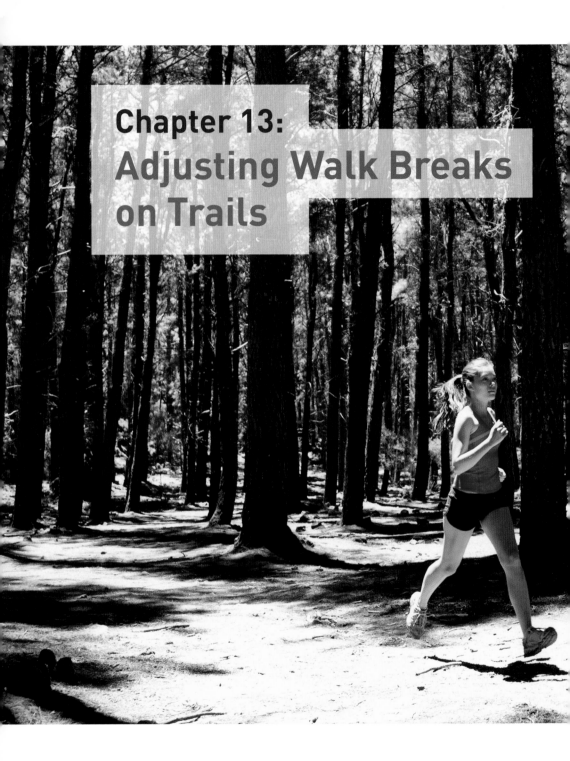

Chapter 13:
Adjusting Walk Breaks on Trails

Walk breaks are even more important on long trail runs than on long pavement runs. Not only will the walks allow you to cope with trail hazards, at the end of a trail run your legs are going to be tired and less able to respond to uneven challenges. I hear from quite a few runners every year who tell me that they could have avoided falls, ankle injuries, and tree impact injuries if they had taken walk breaks more frequently.

© Thinkstock/iStock

65

Using a Run-Walk-Run timer on smooth sections can help you settle into a rhythm. Our Blue Mountain Beach, Florida retreat has mile after mile of mostly stable surface trails, and we use timers. Many runners who don't take the walks according to a rhythm in the beginning tend to get more tired by the end of the run. Even if you don't feel like you need to take a walk break during the first mile or two, your legs will thank you later if you do so.

On most trails, the walk breaks will be taken as needed, as noted next. Because you are facing unknown footing ahead on most trails, it's best to walk at the first sign of a hazard. On rugged trails, watch for rough terrain, slippery surfaces, unknown surfaces, and frequent holes. By walking before you get into risky footing you not only reduce your rate of injury—you allow the muscles to recover before severe fatigue sneaks up on you. In the process, you gain control over your run.

Running form can help you stay under control and stable. Shorten your stride down to baby steps if needed. Keep your feet underneath you at all times. As long as you clear the obstacles on the ground, don't bounce off the ground. A light touch of the foot, using these form suggestions can allow you to slow down, stop, or make side-to-side movements more easily when needed.

Walk through uneven surfaces. Be prepared at any time to slow down and walk. Keep looking ahead, sizing up the potential surface issues. Always err on the side of walking or even stopping to ensure you have stable ground. When leaves and other debris cover the trail, walk carefully until you feel the path is secure.

Slippery when wet! Moisture can make dirt, rocks, and rock faces very slick. Walk carefully through areas that could be risky. When a stream covers the trail, walk around to find a narrow place to cross. If you have to cross the stream, it's usually better to walk through it because you don't know if the ground underneath the water.

Walk up steep hills. It is not only more difficult to run up a hill, you can't see the surface ahead as well as when running on the flat. It only takes one patch of loose gravel to send you crashing down the hill. When in doubt, be extra careful.

Beware when tired: Take extra time to stay under control. At the end of a long run, you will not be able to control feet and legs as you can when fresh. When rocks, slippery surface, and holes are present, you're more likely to get injured if you try to run through the hazards.

Primary concept of walk breaks is the same on trails as on pavement: If you take them early and more frequently, you will have better muscle control, more energy, and quicker reflex action later. Even if you have run a trail a hundred times, weather and nature can present you with challenges you did not anticipate. You want to have as many resources as possible when challenged.

Chapter 14:
Running Form

I believe that running is an inertia activity: Your mission is simply to run smooth and maintain momentum. Very little strength is needed to run. The first few strides get you into motion, and your focus thereafter is to stay in motion. To reduce fatigue, aches, and pains, your body intuitively fine-tunes your motion so that you minimize effort as you continue to run, month after month.

When we run on pavement, we often rely on our feet to adjust the momentum of our stride if we get out of balance. Because of unknown surfaces and uneven terrain, your feet may be at risk if you use the same balance techniques used on pavement. The result is a spill on the dirt or rocks or an injury.

While you want to use the many biomechanical adaptations for running and walking passed down by our ancestors, to avoid mishaps it's best to make several slight form adjustments. Some of these are so subtle that you may not notice them. You can reduce injury risk and enjoy the trail more if you try the following and use the ones that work for you.

Let the ankle do most of the work. The anatomical origin of efficiency in humans is the combination of the ankle, the calf muscle, and the Achilles tendon. This is an extremely sophisticated system of levers, springs, balancing devices and more, involving hundreds of component parts that are amazingly well coordinated. Biomechanics experts believe that this degree of development was not needed for walking. When our ancient ancestors had to run to survive, the evolution reached a new level of performance.

Calf muscle used only when needed: When a runner develops efficient running form and uses the right balance of walking and running, very little effort from the calf muscle produces a smooth continuation of forward movement. As the calf muscle gets in better shape, and you apply the right Run-Walk-Run strategy, you can keep going, mile after mile, with little perceived effort. Other muscle groups offer support and fine-tune the process. When you feel aches and pains that might be due to the way you run, going back to the minimal use of the ankle and Achilles tendon can often leave you feeling smooth and efficient very quickly.

Reducing stride length and staying low to the ground will reduce effort and injury risk. This motion relies on the ankle and reduces fatigue in the calf muscle and is the main reason why runners slow down at the end of races. This minimal motion will allow you to gain more control as you approach trail hazards. You can move into a walk or stop more easily. You'll also reduce injury risk of Achilles tendon and calf muscle.

A better way of running on trails

Most of the runners I've worked with who have struggled with trail form issues have found solutions by making small changes in form. When running within your most conservative range of motion, the legs will have more strength at the end of trail runs and more energy after long ones. There will also be fewer aches and pains. According to the research, most runners are not far from their highest level of efficiency. I believe this is due to the action of the right brain in the frontal lobe. After tens of thousands of steps, it keeps searching for (and then refines) the most efficient pattern of feet, legs, and body alignment.

In my full-day running schools and weekend retreats, I conduct an individual running form analysis with each runner. After having analyzed over ten thousand runners, I've also found that most are running in a very efficient way. The problems are seldom big ones, but rather a series of small mistakes. By making a few minor adjustments, most runners can feel better on every trail run.

The big three: Posture, stride, and bounce

In these consultations, I've also discovered that when runners have problems, they tend to occur in three areas: posture, stride, and bounce. The problems tend to be specific in nature. They occur most often in certain areas because of specific motions. Fatigue increases the irritation of the "weak link" areas. A slight over-stride, for example creates fatigue and then a feeling of weakness at the end of a run. As a tired body "wobbles," other muscle groups try to keep the body on course, even though they are not designed for this. One may fall or irritate the ankle, iliotibial band, Achilles tendon, or other "weak links."

Five negative results of inefficient form:

- Fatigue becomes so severe that it takes much longer to recover.
- Muscles are pushed so far beyond their limits that they break down and get injured.
- The experience is so negative that the desire to run is reduced, producing burnout.
- The "weak links" in your body become over-used and break.
- There are more stumbles, stepping in holes, and compensation injuries on trails.

I've not seen anyone run with perfect form, which is specific to the individual anyway. I don't suggest that everyone should try to run perfectly because we have many adaptations based upon our unique range of motion. But when you become aware of your form problems and make changes to keep them from producing aches and pains, you'll experience fewer aches, smoother running, and faster times. This chapter can help you understand why aches and pains tend to come out of form problems—and how you may be able to reduce or eliminate them.

If you feel relaxed and running is easy even at the end of a run, you're probably running correctly.

Overall, the running motion should feel smooth, relaxed, and easy most of the time. There should be no tension in your neck, back, shoulders or legs. If you are experiencing some issues of this type, posture or foot and leg placement

© Thinkstock/ Digital Vision / Janie Airey

is often the cause. Don't try to run through tightness or pain; try to adjust your running motion, with a few more walk breaks, so that the symptoms go away.

Posture

Good trail running posture is actually good body posture. The head is naturally balanced over the shoulders, which are aligned over the hips. As the foot comes underneath, all of these elements are in balance so that no energy is needed to prop up the body. You shouldn't have to work to pull a wayward body back from a wobble or inefficient motion. You are in command over the next segment of the trail when you are upright.

Forward lean

The posture errors tend to be mostly due to a forward lean—especially when we are tired. The head stretches ahead, which often produces a faster pace that can get one out of control on trails. Beginners often lean to look at every detail of the trail when running instead of walking to regain control. This results in more than a few falls on the trail. A forward lean will often concentrate fatigue, pain, and tightness in the lower back or neck, which goes away when running upright.

It all starts with the head. When the neck muscles are relaxed, the head is usually in a natural position. If there is tension in the neck, or soreness afterward, the head is usually leaning too far forward. This triggers a more general upper-body imbalance in which the head and chest are suspended slightly ahead of the hips and feet. Ask a running companion to tell you if and when your head is too far forward or leaning down. The ideal position of the head is mostly upright, with your eyes focused about 30-40 yards ahead of you.

Most runners I've worked with and observed (even at the world-class level) run more efficiently and with less pain in a relatively upright body posture. There are a few runners I meet each year who have genetic spinal or other issues and naturally lean forward. In this case, each runner should do what is natural for him or her.

Sitting back

The hips are the other major postural component that can get out of alignment. A runner with this problem, when observed from the side, will have the butt behind the rest of the body. When the pelvis area is shifted back, the legs are not allowed to go through a natural range of motion, and the stride length becomes shorter with a slowdown in the pace. Many runners tend to hit harder on their heels when their hips are shifted back. There is less control over balance in this position—causing falls on the trail.

Backward lean

A backward lean for runners is rare, but it happens. In my experience, this is usually due to a structural problem in the spine or hips. If you do this, and you're having pain in the neck, back, or hips, you should see an orthopedist. Those who run with a backward lean on trails should walk more than they run and be vigilant.

Correction: "Puppet on a string"

The best correction I've found to postural problems has been this mental exercise: Imagine that you are a puppet on a string. Suspended from up above like a puppet—from the head and each side of the shoulders—your head lines up with the shoulders, the hips come directly underneath, and the feet naturally touch lightly. It won't hurt anyone to do the "puppet" several times during a run.

It helps to combine this image with a deep breath and mental exercise: About every 4-5 minutes as you start to run after a walk break, take a deep, lower lung breath, straighten up and say "I'm a puppet." Then imagine that you don't have to spend energy maintaining this upright posture because the strings attached from above keep you on track. As you continue to do this, you reinforce good posture as you produce a good habit.

Upright posture not only allows you to stay relaxed, but will also react well to terrain changes, so insert walk breaks when needed and avoid trail problems. Those who lean forward tend to be more unstable on an uneven surface.

An oxygen dividend

Breathing improves when you straighten up. A leaning body can't get ideal use out of the lower lungs. This can cause side pain. When you run upright, the lower lungs can receive adequate air, absorb the oxygen better, and reduce the chance of side pain.

Feet low to the ground

The most efficient stride is a shuffle—with feet next to the ground. Obviously you need to watch the surface and get over the trail hazards. But minimal clearance will reduce energy use and lower muscle fatigue. Staying low to the ground will also reduce pounding of the foot. Most runners don't need more

© Thinkstock/iStock

than one inch (2 1/2 cm) clearance and adapt well after several trail runs. In the beginning, however, it's best to take walk breaks at the sight of any debris on the trail.

Your ankle and the Achilles tendon will act as a spring, moving you forward on each running step. If you stay low to the ground, very little effort is required. Through this shuffling technique, running becomes almost automatic. When runners err on bounce, they try to push off too hard. This can irritate the Achilles tendon and increase calf muscle fatigue. You'll use unnecessary effort as you lift the body off the ground. Think of this as energy wasted in the air, energy that could be used to run another mile or two.

The other negative force that penalizes those with a higher bounce is gravity. The higher you rise, the harder you will fall. Each additional bounce off the ground delivers a lot more impact on feet and legs—which on trail runs can lead to foot pain and instability.

Correcting too much bounce: Light touch

The ideal foot placement should be so light that you don't feel yourself pushing off or landing. This means that your foot stays low to the ground and goes through an efficient and natural motion. Instead of trying to overcome gravity, you are in synch with it.

Here's a light touch drill: Pick a stable segment of a familiar trail. During the middle of a run, time yourself for 20 seconds. Focus on one item: touching so softly that you don't hear your feet. Earplugs are not allowed for this drill. Imagine that you are running on thin ice or through a bed of hot coals. Do several of these 20-second touches, becoming quieter and quieter. You should feel very little impact on your feet as you do this drill.

Stride length

Studies have shown that a shorter stride is more efficient for distance runners. Trail runners find that shorter strides give them more control over their momentum, balance, and adjustments to uneven terrain.

A major cause of aches, pains, and injuries is a stride that is too long. But when in doubt, it is always better to err on the side of having a shorter stride.

Don't lift your knees— especially when running uphill!

Even world-class distance runners don't do this, because it tires the quadriceps muscle (front of the thigh), leading to a stride that is too long to be efficient. The most common time when runners stride too long is at the end of a tiring run. This slight over-stride when the legs are tired will leave your quads (front of thigh) sore the next day or two.

Don't kick out too far in front of you!

If you watch the natural movement of the leg, it will kick forward slightly as the foot gently moves forward in the running motion to contact the ground. Let this be a natural motion that produces no tightness in the muscles behind the lower or upper leg.

Tightness in the front of the shin, or behind the knee, or in the hamstring (back of the thigh) is a sign that you are kicking too far forward. Correct this by staying low to the ground, shortening the stride, and lightly touching the ground.

Cadence drill (CD)

This easy cadence drill improves your efficiency, making running easier. This CD helps you to pull all the elements of good running form together at the same time. Over the weeks and months, if you do this drill once every week, you will find that your normal cadence slowly increases naturally and you tend to run more smoothly.

- Do this drill on a very secure segment of trail or paved surface.
- Warm up by walking for 5 minutes and then running and walking very gently for 10 minutes.
- Start jogging slowly for 1-2 minutes, and time yourself for 30 seconds. During this half-minute, count the number of times your left foot touches.
- Walk around for a minute or so.
- On the second 30-second drill, increase the count by 1 or 2.
- Repeat this three to seven more times. Each time trying to increase by one to two additional counts.
- The Galloway Run-Walk-Run timer (visit www.JeffGalloway.com) makes it easy to keep track of the 30-second interval.

In the process of improving turnover, the body's internal monitoring system coordinates a series of adaptations which pulls together all of the form components into an efficient team:

- Your foot touches more gently.
- Extra, inefficient motions of the foot and leg are reduced or eliminated.
- Less effort is spent on pushing up or pushing forward.
- You stay lower to the ground.
- The ankle becomes more efficient.
- Ache and pain areas are not overused.

Walking form

Walking form is usually not an issue when walking at a gentle, strolling pace. But every year, I hear from several runners who are injured because they are walking in a way that irritates some area of the foot or leg. Most of these problems come from trying to walk too fast, with too long a stride, or from using a race walking or power walking technique.

- Avoid a long walking stride. Top priority for trail runners is to stay balanced. A long stride gets one out of balance.
- Maintain a relaxed motion that does not stress the knees, tendons, or muscles of the leg, feet, knees, or hips. If you feel pain or irritation in these areas, shorten your stride. Many runners find that they can learn to walk fairly fast with a short stride. But when in doubt, use the walk for recovery and ease off.
- Don't lead with your arms. Minimal arm swing is best. Swinging the arms too much can encourage a longer walk stride, which can push you into aches and pains quickly. The extra rotation produced can also irritate hip, shoulder, and neck areas. You want the legs to set the rhythm for your walk and your run. When this happens you are more likely to get into the "zone" of the right brain hemisphere.
- Let your feet move the way that is natural for you. When runners or walkers try techniques that are unnatural for them, the usual result is aches, pains, and injuries.

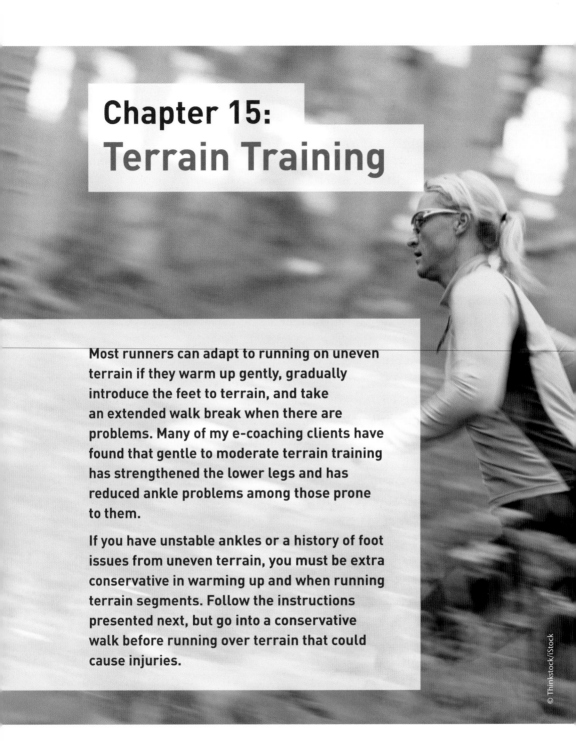

Chapter 15:
Terrain Training

Most runners can adapt to running on uneven terrain if they warm up gently, gradually introduce the feet to terrain, and take an extended walk break when there are problems. Many of my e-coaching clients have found that gentle to moderate terrain training has strengthened the lower legs and has reduced ankle problems among those prone to them.

If you have unstable ankles or a history of foot issues from uneven terrain, you must be extra conservative in warming up and when running terrain segments. Follow the instructions presented next, but go into a conservative walk before running over terrain that could cause injuries.

© Thinkstock/iStock

Once your feet, legs, and muscles have adapted to uneven terrain, regular runs on grass, fields, and trails will maintain these adaptations. At least one day a week, during one of your short runs, find a stable area of grass or dirt, and run gently for two to four segments of about five minutes each.

Warm up by walking for three to five minutes on stable terrain. Staying on stable terrain, do a gentle warm up with more walking than you plan to use later for five minutes. During the next five minutes, still on stable terrain, gradually ease into the Run-Walk-Run strategy that you will be using later in the run. If all is well, begin your terrain segment with 20-30 seconds on stable grass or dirt, followed by 30-60 seconds of gentle walking to allow the feet and ankles to adapt. Continue to alternate segments three to four times, gradually increasing the roughness of the terrain until it simulates the type of terrain you want to prepare for. Don't get into an uncomfortable situation. Walk gently for two to three minutes and start over again, gradually increasing the roughness of the terrain.

At first you should do only five minutes of these segments. Gradually increase the number of segments until you are doing 5-10 x 5-minute segments. This allows the feet, ankles, and legs to adapt to uneven terrain.

Don't keep running on terrain that could produce injury. Structure the terrain segment so that you have a stable area within a few steps and move to that area when needed. Don't hesitate to walk as much as needed between terrain segments.

There is no need to run over very rocky and risky terrain. Even in races, you should walk gently through such areas.

If you have not run on uneven terrain for several weeks, ease back into this by using the starter workout first. Those who have problems with unstable terrain need to be careful and should use an even more conservative approach to the terrain than suggested previously. All runners should run these terrain segments slowly during the first few workouts.

Chapter 16:
Hill Training

© Jeff Galloway

Top mistakes made when running hills on trails

1. Striding too long down a hill
2. Striding too long up a hill
3. Increasing the pace when running up a hill
4. Leaning too far forward when running up a hill
5. Leaning too far back when running down a hill
6. Leaning too far forward when running down a hill
7. Pumping the arms to get up a hill faster
8. Trying to "win the hill"
9. Not taking strategic walk breaks when running up or down a hill

Hill running concepts

1. Keep the effort level and breathing rate consistent and conversational as you approach a hill.
2. Touch lightly as you go up the hill (many trail runners walk up most or all hills).
3. If you insert running segments when going uphill, reduce stride length as you run up to maintain resiliency in the leg muscles.
4. Reduce stride to baby steps when needed on steep hills or long hills—OR WALK.
5. Monitor effort by breathing rate; try to maintain the same breathing pattern as on the flat.
6. Stay smooth when running up and running down.
7. Let gravity pull you down the hill as you touch lightly with a relatively short stride.
8. Let cadence or turnover increase as you run down, without a great increase in stride length.
9. Watch for trail hazards constantly and walk through them.
10. Don't over-stride!

Uphill running form

- Start with a fairly short comfortable stride.
- As you go up the hill, shorten the stride further.
- Touch lightly with your feet.
- Maintain a body posture that is perpendicular to the horizontal (upright, not leaning forward or back).
- Pick up the turnover of your feet as you go up and over the top.
- Keep adjusting your stride so that the leg muscles don't tighten up; you want them as resilient as possible.
- Relax as you go over the top of the hill, and glide (or coast) on the downside, minimizing effort.

Downhill form

- Maintain a light touch of the foot.
- Use an average stride, or a quick shuffle.
- Keep feet low to the ground.
- Let gravity pull you down the hill.
- Turnover of the feet will pick up.
- Try to glide (or coast) quickly down the hill.
- Take strategic walk breaks if you feel the need.

Hill training for strength and race preparation

Even if your next trail race is on relatively flat terrain, you will encounter a hill at some point.

Hill training is the best leg strengthening exercise for any type of running. By doing a regular series of hill workouts you can develop the foot and leg adaptations needed for running various types of hills.

With the added strength from hill training, one can adjust to an efficient stride, run more efficiently and reduce wear and tear on the muscles at the end of all runs. You'll also improve your hill running technique in races.

The hill-training workouts are not designed to result in exhaustion. They should gently introduce the feet, legs and cardiovascular system to uphills and downhills, while improving muscle strength and running efficiency.

Terrain

The main benefits of hill training, listed above, can be achieved by running hills on paved surfaces, such as sidewalks, park asphalt trails, streets, overpasses, and bridges. It would also help to do a few hill sessions on the type of terrain you will encounter in your race.

Walking hills in races

Even if you plan to walk the hills in your trail race, it is wise to do a hill workout every 7-14 days. Just run up and down a hill that is 50-100 yards long. Start with 2-3 of these hills and increase by 1-2 each workout until you are doing 8-10 hills. If you anticipate some longer hills in your race, find longer hills once you have increased the number of hill repetitions to 8.

The hill workout

- Walk for 2-3 minutes.
- Jog and walk to a hill—about 10 minutes. Beginners should jog a minute and walk a minute (a longer warm-up is fine) during the first few weeks of training.
- Reverse this warm-up for your cool-down.
- Choose a hill with an easy or moderate grade—steep hills often cause problems.

- Run up the hill for 5 seconds, and then down for 5 seconds, gently. Walk for 15-20 seconds. Repeat this 5-10 times. This finalizes the warm-up.
- Walk for 3-4 minutes.
- Run the first few steps of each hill acceleration at a jog; then gradually pick up the turnover of the feet as you go up the hill.
- Get into a comfortable rhythm so that you can gradually increase this turnover (number of steps per minute) as you go up the hill.
- Keep shortening stride length as you go up the hill.
- It's okay to huff and puff at the top of the hill (due to increased turnover and running uphill), but don't let the legs get over extended, or feel exhausted.
- Run over the top of the hill by at least four steps.
- Jog back to the top of the hill and walk down to recover between the hills. Walk as much as you need for complete recovery after each hill.

Hill workout running form

- Start with a fairly comfortable stride.
- As you go up the hill, shorten the stride.
- Touch lightly with your feet.
- Maintain a body posture that is upright, not leaning forward or back.
- Pick up the turnover of your feet as you go up and over the top.
- Keep adjusting stride so that the leg muscles don't tighten up; you want them as resilient as possible.
- Relax as you go over the top of the hill, and glide (or coast) a bit on the way down.

Strengthening lower legs and improving running form through hill training

The incline of the hill forces your legs to work harder as you ascend. The extra work up the incline and the faster turnover build strength. By taking an easy walk between the hills and an easy day afterward, the lower leg muscles rebuild stronger. Over several months, the improved strength allows you to support your bodyweight farther forward on your feet. An extended range of motion of the ankle and Achilles tendon results in a "bonus" extension of the foot forward—with no increase in effort. You will run faster without working harder. What a deal!

© Thinkstock/iStock

Running faster on hills in races

Top priority is to save resources when going uphill in races—especially during the first half. When in doubt, walk most or all of the uphills.

Once you train yourself to run with efficient hill form, you'll build the strength to handle any hill and gain more confidence when you encounter hills during a race. Hill training allows you to cruise up a hill without the degree of huffing and puffing that you used to experience. In other words, hill workouts will make running uphill almost as natural as running on the flat. When you come to a hill in a race, you won't have to work as hard and can save resources for the end of the race. As your technique gets better through hill training, you will also be able to run faster than you used to run up the same hill on a racecourse. Those who used to walk up every hill have been able to run segments of hills after hill training.

Hill technique in a race is the same as in workouts: Keep shortening your stride as you move up the hill. Monitor your respiration rate; don't huff and puff more than you were doing on the flat. As runners improve their hill technique in races, they find that a shorter and quicker stride reduces effort while increasing speed. This is particularly beneficial during the last half of a hilly trail course. Your stride is short enough when there is no increase in breathing rate. When in doubt, use baby steps and insert more walking.

Note: On your long runs and the first half of trail races, just walk or insert more walk breaks on the uphill portions. If your breathing increases on a hill, reduce effort and stride length until your respiration is as it was on the flat ground, or take more frequent walk breaks.

Making the biggest mistakes: Too long a stride or bouncing too much

Even if the stride is one or two inches too long, your downhill speed can get out of control. If you are bouncing more than an inch or two off the ground, you run the risk of pounding your feet, having to use your quads to slow down (producing soreness), and creating hamstring soreness due to over-stride. The best indicator of over-stride is having tight hamstrings (big muscles behind your upper legs) and sore quads the next day. Using a quick and slightly shorter stride allows you to run just as fast downhill, avoiding the long stride and eliminating sore quads, sore shins, and aggravated hamstrings.

Chapter 17:
Choosing a Goal

Before choosing a race distance, it's best to determine what you want to get out of your running over the next 6-12 months. Make a list of priorities. For me, top priority is to enjoy every run. Before I choose a goal, I make sure that I have a great chance of accomplishing #1.

© Thinkstock/Digital Vision

Next, you want to look at the type of events that might be of interest to you. There are several factors that could influence your decision: event distance, location, travel required, your schedule, course beauty, or hazards on the course that could aggravate injuries.

Search the Internet for races of various distances. A great website for marathons, for example, is www.marathonguide.com. When you find races that look interesting, read the runner reviews. They are usually quite revealing.

Here are some goals that trail runners find interesting:

1. Be able to run on gentle trails without injury: The two goals are to experience the joy and beauty of trail running while avoiding rough terrain and other conditions that could produce injury. The number of trails in this category is relatively small and can be verified by veteran trail runners. Be sure to check out the elevation profile.

2. Enjoy various trails, a variety of terrain, different surfaces, in a variety of weather conditions: You may choose one or more of the elements to suit your current desires. This expands possibilities while increasing the odds of aches and pains.

3. Run in trail races to finish: As you go through the selection process, look at the time allowed to officially finish. Then, do the "Magic Mile" and compute your potential in the marathon. On very rough 5K and 10K courses, the per-mile pace is often marathon-pace or slightly slower. On very rough half marathon courses, add 1-2 minutes per mile to projected marathon potential. Tough marathon courses should receive an adjustment of 3-4 minutes per mile slower than current marathon potential. Ultra marathons tend to slow one down by 4-6 minutes per mile, depending upon the terrain.

4. Improve time in races: Time improvement requires longer long runs, the addition of speed training, fine-tuning of Run-Walk-Run, and terrain training. See chapter 23, Faster Trail Racing.

Computing pace by kilometer

Note: To find per kilometer pace, convert mile pace to a decimal and multiply by .62. For example, 10:24 per mile would be 10.4 x .62 = 6.448 which is = 6:27/km

Training program guidelines

1. The following programs are designed for those who have already been running regularly but have never run a race at the current goal distance. They are also designed for veterans who don't have a time goal.
2. On long runs, and the race itself, slow down when the temperature rises above 60 °F (14 °C) by 30 seconds a mile for every 5 degrees above 60 °F or more. (20 sec/km slower for every 2 °C above 14 °C)
3. Be sure to take a break from strenuous exercise the day before your weekend runs.
4. Terrain training is noted on each schedule. Read chapter 15 for more information on terrain training. Parks, forest trails, and other areas are possible venues. If you know the type of terrain you will be running in the race, try to run on similar terrain several times before the race.

Training strategy

Whether you are just trying to get through a tough trail run or race or have a time goal, you need a strategy and a plan. Trail running involves surface changes, elevation, weather, trail hazards, and more. Preparing adequately, therefore, means planning the training elements, trying out equipment, getting on the trails during adverse weather, and constantly thinking ahead.

As always, put safety first. Walk and keep your feet firmly planted. Follow the advice on the trail challenges in chapter 9. Most serious trail injuries are due to falls. If you keep your feet stable, you'll have a chance to avoid serious impact injuries.

Distance runs: These can be run mostly on smooth surface. The primary planning issue is scheduling the long ones so that you will have the time needed to complete these long runs. See the training schedules chapter for more information.

Uneven surface training: I suggest to devote at least one day a week to running for at least 20 minutes on various trail surfaces. This will allow you to be ready for just about any challenge, as your feet and legs adapt.

Hill training: If you expect to be challenged by uphills and downhills on trail races or treks, it is crucial to do some hill training. Try to simulate the types of hills you will experience on the course as much as possible. Even if you don't know the course and can only run hills on pavement, regular hill workouts will strengthen the legs and improve your ability to cope with the ups and downs of the race. Read the chapter 16 on hill training.

Combining terrain and hill training: At least every 14 days it is beneficial to run a hill workout on trails. As always, be careful as you run and walk when there are hazards. Your body will adapt better to hilly trails if you run some hilly trail segments.

Previewing race course: If at all possible, go to the trail area and run the course. Some run the trail in segments. Others concentrate on the more difficult portions, the areas where runners tend to get lost, and the last fourth of the trail race. Knowing how far you are from the finish or other landmarks bestows a huge psychological advantage in a race.

Weather training: The challenges of trail running usually increase when there is adverse weather. Dirt trails and rocky trails become more slippery and sandy surfaces becomes more solid. Some trails will fill up with water throughout low-lying areas with minimal drainage. The best strategy is to be prepared.

The "Magic Mile" time trials (MM) are reality checks on your goal. These should be done on the weeks noted on the schedule. The MM has been the best predictor of current potential and helps to set a realistic training pace.

With this information, you can decide how hard to run during various situations. (If you have any injuries you should not do the MM)

- Warm up for these with about 10 minutes of very easy running with liberal walk breaks.
- Do 4-6 accelerations as in the book—no sprinting.
- Run around a track if at all possible (or a very accurately measured segment).
- Time yourself for 4 laps (or an accurately measured mile). Start the watch at the beginning, and keep it running until you cross the finish of the 4th lap.
- On the first MM, don't run all-out: run at a pace that is only slightly faster than your current pace.
- Only one MM is done on each day it is assigned.
- On each successive MM (usually 3 weeks later), your mission is to beat the previous best time.

© Thinkstock/iStock

- Don't ever push so hard that you hurt your feet, knees, etc.
- Jog slowly for the rest of the distance assigned on that day taking as many walk breaks as you wish.
- At the end of the program, take your fastest MM and multiply by 1.3 to see what pace might be possible on an ideal day in a trail half marathon, with average degree of rocks, roots, etc.
- Training pace is at least two minutes per mile slower than this (MM x 1.3) pace.

After you have run 3 of these MMs (not at one time—on different weekends) you'll see progress and will run them hard enough so that you are huffing and puffing during the second half. For prediction purposes, you want to finish, feeling like you couldn't go much further at that pace. Try walking for about 10-15 seconds at the half during the MM. Some runners record a faster time when taking short breaks, and some go faster when running continuously. Do what works for you on the MM.

Chapter 18:
5K Training

Goal: To finish injury free

© Jeff Galloway

Time required: 30 minutes on two weekdays (Tue/Thu or Mon/Wed) plus one weekend run/walk that will build gradually to 3.5 miles. Walk-breaks can eliminate or reduce excessive fatigue or orthopedic stress.

Who: This program is designed for those who have been running about 20 minutes, two to three days a week for at least two months, who are not interested in a time goal. The advice is given as one exerciser to another. For medical issues, see a doctor.

Textbook: My book *5K/10K Running* has more information on both of these events. You can order this book, autographed, from www. JeffGalloway.com.

Walkers: Simply follow the schedule provided next. Walk slowly on all of the long ones. I don't recommend power walking or race walking.

Use a short stride: Whether walking or running, adjust your stride to be relaxed and well within a natural range of motion for you. Keep your feet low to the ground. Shorter strides reduce effort and orthopedic stress.

The long one: Run these endurance runs on terrain that is as flat as possible in your area and on a stable, paved surface. Insert liberal walk breaks from the beginning. As you push back the length of the long run, every two weeks, you'll extend endurance limits, improve mental concentration at the end of races, and enhance your physiological infrastructure. Longer long run/walks, for example, improve your cardiovascular system to deliver blood better to the exercising muscles and withdraw waste more effectively. The endurance workout is the primary training component in a 5K program. For those who have run a 5K before, and want to run faster, see the [TG = __] for recommended distance.

Long run pace must be slow: I've developed a simple 800-meter test to determine a recommended pace for the long run. Go to a track and run very slowly for two laps. Take as many walk breaks as you need to avoid huffing and puffing on this test. If you are not huffing and puffing at the end of the second lap, take your time, multiply by two and add three minutes. If you are huffing and puffing at the end, multiply by two and add four minutes. The result is the fastest per mile time you should be recording on your long runs; you can always go slower. These tests are noted on the weekend schedule as (800T). Run/walk gently for 10 minutes before timing yourself for the 800. Only one 800 is timed during each of these workouts. Jog and walk gently for the rest of the time for that workout. You can adjust your long run pace as the 800T time improves.

Examples:
1 800 time is 6:00 without huffing and puffing: 6:00 X 2 = 12:00. Adding 3 minutes will give you a long run pace of no faster than 15 min/mile.
2 800 time is 6:00 but you are huffing and puffing at the end: 6 X 2 = 12:00. Adding 4 minutes will give you a long run pace of no faster than 16 minutes/mile.

Note: It is always okay to run slower than the pace calculated from this time trial.

Run-Walk-Run: This method has allowed hundreds of thousands of beginners to finish races of 5K and longer distances. By inserting a walk break right from the beginning of the workout and continuing to walk according to a plan, there is no need to experience extra fatigue, pain, or injuries. For more information visit www.JeffGalloway.com.

Long run strategy: The amount of running and walking is adjusted for the pace per mile. After running the 800-meter test and calculating the long run pace, use the table in chapter 12 as your guide.

Maintenance workouts: Usually the long workout is done on weekends and the two maintenance workouts are done on Tuesday and Thursday (or Monday and Wednesday when the long one is on Saturday). During the middle of one or both of these maintenance workouts, you can do the terrain training as noted in this book.

The pace of these can be as slow or as fast as you want to go, as long as you are recovering well from the weekend long ones. Beware of fast running as this increases the risk of aches, pains, and injuries.

Rest days: When you go farther than you have gone before, your muscles, tendons, and joints need time to rebuild stronger. Take the day off from exercise the day before and after a long one. On the other non-running days, you can do any exercise that does not fatigue the calf muscles. So walking, swimming, cycling, elliptical, and rowing are fine. But stair machines, leg weight work, and step aerobics are not.

Warm up: Walk for 3 minutes, then run for 15-30 seconds and walk for the rest of the 3-5 minutes. Then use the Run-Walk-Run strategy that is appropriate.

Cool down: After your workout, don't stop. Jog slowly, using as many walk breaks as you wish for the next 10 minutes, and then walk for 3-5 minutes. Then you're done!

If you are already running more than two miles, you can start at the week on the schedule that is equal to or less than the length of the longest run you have done in the past two weeks. If you have not finished a long one of two miles or longer within the last three weeks, go very slowly and complete a two-mile workout before starting this program—even if you have to walk it.

Terrain training: Do the terrain training that is mentioned in chapter 15.

Note: At www.JeffGalloway.com you can find a timer that will beep or vibrate to tell you when to walk and when to run.

[TG = __] (TG = Time Goal) is the recommendation for 5K veterans who want to run faster this season.

The Schedule:

Week 1: Tuesday 20 min (800T), Thursday 23 min, Saturday 2 mile [TG = 4 mi]

Week 2: Tuesday 26 min, Thursday 29 min, Saturday 30 min (800T)

Week 3: Tuesday 30 min, Thursday 30 min, Saturday 2.5 mi [TG = 5.5 mi]

Week 4: Tuesday 30 min, Thursday 30 min, Saturday 30 min (800T)

Week 5: Tuesday 30 min, Thursday 30 min, Saturday 3 mi [TG = 7 mi]

Week 6: Tuesday 30 min, Thursday 30 min, Saturday 30 min (800T)

Week 7: Tuesday 30 min, Thursday 30 min, Saturday 3.5 mi [TG = 8.5 mi]

Week 8: Tuesday 30 min, Thursday 30 min, Saturday 40 min (800T)

Week 9: Tuesday 30 min, Thursday 30 min, Saturday 4 mi [TG = 10 mi]

Week 10: Tuesday 30 min, Thursday 30 min, Saturday 30 min

Week 11: Tuesday 30 min, Thursday 30 min, Saturday 5K Race!

Week 12: Tuesday 30 min, Thursday 30 min, Saturday 30 min

Chapter 19:
10K Training

Goal: To finish, injury free

© Thinkstock/iStock

Time required: 30 minutes on two weekdays (Tue/Thu or Mon/Wed) plus one weekend run/walk that will build gradually to 6.5 miles. Walk breaks can eliminate or reduce excessive fatigue or orthopedic stress.

Who: This program is designed for those who have been running about 20 minutes, 2-3 days a week for at least two months, who are not interested in a time goal, and who have completed a 5K or a three-mile run. If you have not run this far, use the 5K training program on www.JeffGalloway.com. The advice is given as one exerciser to another. For medical issues, see a doctor.

Textbook: My book *5K/10K Running* has more information on both of these events. You can order this book on www.JeffGalloway.com.

Walkers: Simply follow the schedule provided next. Walk slowly on all of the long ones. I don't recommend power-walking or race-walking.

Use a short stride: Whether walking or running, adjust your stride so that it is relaxed and well within a natural range of motion for you. Keep the feet low to the ground. Shorter strides reduce effort and orthopedic stress.

The long one: Run these endurance runs on terrain that is as flat as you have in your area. Insert liberal walk-breaks from the beginning. As you push back the length of the long run, every two weeks, you'll extend endurance limits, improve mental concentration at the end of races, and enhance your physiological infrastructure. Longer long run/walks, for example, improve your cardiovascular system to deliver blood better to the exercising muscles and withdraw waste more effectively. The endurance workout is the primary training component in a 10K program. It is best to do the long ones on a stable, paved surface. For those who have run a 10K before and want to run faster, see the [TG = __] for recommended distance.

The long run pace must be slow: I've developed a simple 800-meter test to determine a recommended pace for the long run. Go to a track and run very slowly for two laps. Take as many walk breaks as you need to avoid huffing and puffing on this test. If you are not huffing and puffing at the end of the second lap, take your time, multiply by two and add three minutes. If you are huffing and puffing at the end, multiply by two and add four minutes. The result is the fastest per-mile time you should be recording on your long runs; you can always go slower.

These tests are noted on the weekend schedule as (800T). Run/walk gently for 10 minutes before timing yourself for the 800. Only one 800 is timed during each of these workouts. Jog and walk gently for the rest of the time for that workout. You can adjust your long run pace as the 800-meter time improves.

Examples:

1 800 time is 6:00 without huffing and puffing: 6:00 X 2 = 12:00. Adding 3 minutes will give you a long run pace of no faster than 15 min/mile.

2 800 time is 6:00 but you are huffing and puffing at the end: 6 X 2 = 12:00. Adding 4 minutes will give you a long run pace of no faster than 16 min/ mile.

Run-Walk-Run: This method has allowed hundreds of thousands of beginners to finish races of 10K and longer distances. If you insert a walk break from the beginning of the workout and continue to walk according to a plan, there is no need to experience extra fatigue, pain, or injuries. See chapter 12 for more information.

Long run strategy: The amount of running and walking is adjusted for the pace per mile. After running the 800-meter test and computing the long run pace, use the table in chapter 12 as your guide.

Maintenance workouts: Usually the long workout is done on weekends, and the two maintenance workouts are done on Tuesday and Thursday (or Monday and Wednesday when the long one is on Saturday). The pace of these can be as slow or as fast as you want to go, as long as you are recovering well from the weekend long ones. Beware of fast running as this increases the risk of aches, pains, and injuries. During the middle of one or both of these maintenance workouts, you can do terrain training, as noted in chapter 15.

Rest days: When you go farther than you have gone before, your muscles, tendons, and joints need time to rebuild stronger. Take the day off from exercise the day before and after a long one. On the other non-running days, you can do any exercise that does not fatigue the calf muscles. So walking, swimming, cycling, elliptical, and rowing are fine. But stair machines, leg weight work, and step aerobics are not.

Warm up: Walk for 3 minutes, then run for 15-30 seconds and walk for the rest of 3-5 minutes. Then use the Run-Walk-Run strategy that is appropriate.

Warm down: After your workout, don't stop. Jog slowly, using as many walk breaks as you wish for the next 10 minutes, and then walk for 3-5 minutes. You're done!

If you are already running more than three miles, you can start at the length of the long run which matches your current long run distance in the past three weeks.

Note: At www.JeffGalloway.com you can find a timer that will beep or vibrate to tell you when to walk and when to run.

[TG = __] is the recommendation for 10K veterans who want to run faster this season

The Schedule:

Week 1: Tuesday 20 min (800T), Thursday 23 min, Saturday 3.5 mile [TG = 4.5 mi]

Week 2: Tuesday 26 min, Thursday 29 min, Saturday 30 min (800T)

Week 3: Tuesday 30 min, Thursday 30 min, Saturday 4 mi [TG = 6 mi]

Week 4: Tuesday 30 min, Thursday 30 min, Saturday 30 min (800T)

Week 5: Tuesday 30 min, Thursday 30 min, Saturday 4.5 mi [TG = 7.5 mi]

Week 6: Tuesday 30 min, Thursday 30 min, Saturday 40 min (800T)

Week 7: Tuesday 30 min, Thursday 30 min, Saturday 5 mi [TG = 9 mi]

Week 8: Tuesday 30 min, Thursday 30 min, Saturday 5K race or timed run

Week 9: Tuesday 30 min, Thursday 30 min, Saturday 5.5 mi [TG = 11 mi]

Week 10: Tuesday 30 min, Thursday 30 min, Saturday 40 min

Week 11: Tuesday 30 min, Thursday 30 min, Saturday 6 mi [TG = 13 mi]

Week 12: Tuesday 30 min, Thursday 30 min, Saturday 40 min

Week 13: Tuesday 30 min, Thursday 30 min, Saturday 6.5 mi [TG = 15 mi]

Week 14: Tuesday 30 min, Thursday 30 min, Saturday 30 min

Week 15: Tuesday 30 min, Thursday 30 min, Saturday 10K Race!

Week 16—Tuesday 30 min, Thursday 30 min, Saturday 30 min

On to the next goal!

Chapter 20:
Half Marathon Training Program

Goal: To finish in the upright position

© Thinkstock/iStock

Welcome to half marathon training! This proven program has led thousands of runners across the finish line, while reducing the chance of injury to almost zero. Only three weekly training days are needed: 30-40 minutes on Tuesday and Thursday and a longer session on the weekend.

The long runs are the key element. As you increase the distance of these (see the following training schedule), endurance barriers are extended to 13.1 miles. You can't go too slowly on the long distance weekends: Your goal is simply to finish each one with strength. Generally, you want to slow down at least three minutes per mile slower than you could currently run a fast marathon. See the Magic Mile section for more information. It's best to run the long runs on stable surface, usually paved. For those who have run a half marathon before and want to run faster, see the [TG = __] for recommended distance.

No huffing and puffing! On long runs, you want to be able to carry on a conversation throughout the run—even at the end. A very slow pace, with liberal walk breaks, will allow almost everyone to feel strong on almost every long one. If you're breathing hard at the end of a long one, you need to adjust to a slower pace with more walk breaks from the beginning of the next one.

Don't be afraid to walk. It's okay to walk the entire distance of long runs. If you missed a long run, you can walk gently for the first half of your next long run and then use the Run-Walk-Run strategy that is appropriate. When challenged at the end of long runs, just walk the rest of the distance.

Running form: Never sprint during a running segment—keep the feet low to the ground, using a light touch and a relatively short stride. Most runners find that an upright posture is best but use what feels natural for you. Let your foot move in the natural way. Most runners naturally land on the heel and gently roll off the midfoot. Those who try to run in a way that is unnatural increase injury risk.

Walking form: Walk with a gentle stride that is relatively short. Power-walking and walking with a long stride increase injury risk.

Slow down in the heat! Surveys have shown that runners tend to slow down 30 seconds/mile for every 5 degrees above 60 °F (20 sec/km slower for every 2 °C above 14 °C). Please make these pace adjustments on hot long run days, using more frequent walk breaks to avoid heat stress. Don't wear a hat on hot days, try to run before the sun rises above the horizon, and pour water over the top of your head to keep cool.

Be sure to check the time limit for the race. The Magic Mile, listed next, can give you guidelines as to the expected finish time, per mile, on the race day. Don't worry if your comfortable long run pace is slower than the pace needed on race day. On at least one run during the week, practice running at a pace that is 30 seconds/mile (20 sec/km) faster than you need to run in the race to get in before the finish line closes—see the following section on race day practice.

By inserting strategic walk breaks from the beginning of long workouts, you can significantly reduce fatigue. The Run-Walk-Run ratio should correspond to the pace used. Suggested strategies can be found in chapter 12. Two maintenance runs, 30-40 minutes each, will sustain the conditioning needed. Most commonly, these are done on Tuesday and Thursday, but any two days between long runs are okay. Each runner can choose the pace or the Run-Walk-Run ratio for each of these runs. It is suggested that you run on uneven terrain for at least part of these runs.

It is fine to walk the entire distance of a long run if there are challenges.

It is fine to do cross-training on Monday, Wednesday, and Friday, if you wish. There will be little benefit to your running in doing this, but you'll improve overall fitness. On the cross-training days, don't do exercises like stair machines that concentrate effort in the calf muscle.

Standard warm-up: Walk for 3-5 minutes; then, run for a few seconds and walk for one to five minutes. Then, gradually increase the amount of running—reducing the amount of walking for five minutes—until you reach the ratio that feels comfortable for you.

Run-Walk-Run practice: On Tuesday, after the standard warm-up, try various Run-Walk-Run strategies. For example, if you are currently running a minute or walking a minute, on your long runs, try a few rotations (3 to 4 min each) of run 30 seconds/walk 30 seconds or 20/20 or 15/15.

Race day practice: On Thursday, after the standard warm-up, time yourself for two miles. Use a Run-Walk-Run strategy that feels comfortable. Try to run at a pace that is 30 seconds per mile faster than finish line closing pace if you suspect that this pace might be a challenge on race day.

Terrain training: Read chapter 15 on terrain training. It is best to devote the middle of one of your short runs each week to this. If you have injuries that could be aggravated by uneven terrain, avoid this training until healing occurs. Terrain training can also be done after the Magic Mile (MM) on the weekends designated for this or combined with Run-Walk-Run practice or race day practice.

Hill training. After your MM, on the designated weekends, you can combine terrain training on hilly terrain, or alternate hill training one MM weekend and terrain the next.

Standard cool-down: Walk for 10 minutes with a gentle and short stride.

Magic Mile (MM): I suggest doing this after the standard warm-up on the non–long-run weekends listed on the schedule. Over the span of the training, you should see steady progress and predict a finish time that is realistic as the race date approaches.
- To convert per mile time into per kilometer time, convert the minutes and seconds into a number with a decimal and then multiply by .62. For example, a 10:00 per mile pace would be 6.2 minutes per kilometer or 6:12 per kilometer.

- This program is the minimum needed to get to the time goal. If you want to run more and do not have aches, pains, or other issues, go ahead.
- **Note:** At www.JeffGalloway.com you can find a timer that will beep or vibrate to tell you when to walk and when to run.

Note: This training advice is given as one runner to another. For medical questions, ask your doctor.

Half marathon training schedule

Goal is to finish in the upright position.

Who: For runners who have been running for at least six months with no time goal.

Three-Day Training Week:
- Tuesday—30-40 minutes (including Run-Walk-Run practice and terrain)
- Thursday—30-40 minutes (including race day practice and terrain)
- Weekend—Listed next

Weekend Workouts
[TG = __] is the recommendation for half marathon veterans who want to run faster this season.

The Schedule:

Week 1: 3 miles [TG = 5 mi]

Week 2: 4 miles [TG = 6.5 mi]

Week 3: 3 miles on trails [TG = 4 x 1/2 mi]

Week 4: 5.5 miles [TG = 8 mi]

Week 5: 3 miles on trails [TG = 6 x 1/2 mi]

Week 6: 7 miles [TG = 10 mi]

Week 7: 4 miles on trails [TG = 8 x 1/2 mi]

Week 8: 9 miles [TG = 12 mi]

Week 9: 4 miles on trails [TG = 10 x 1/2 mi]

Week 10: 11 miles [TG = 14 mi]

Week 11: 4 miles on trails [TG = 12 x 1/2 mi]

Week 12: 13 miles [TG = 16 mi]

Week 13: 4 miles on trails [TG = 14 x 1/2 mi]

Week 14: 14-15 miles [TG = 18 mi]

Week 15: 4 miles on trails

Week 16: Half marathon race

Week 17: 4 miles

Chapter 21:
Marathon Training Program

Goal: To finish in the upright position

Welcome to marathon training! This proven training program has led thousands of runners across the finish line, while reducing the chance of injury to almost zero. Only three weekly training days are needed: 30-40 minutes on Tuesday and Thursday and a longer session on the weekend.

The long runs are the key to marathon training. As you increase the distance of these, you push back your endurance barriers and prepare to go the distance on the race day. You can't go too slowly on the long distance weekends; your goal is simply to finish each one with strength. Generally, you want to slow down at least three minutes per mile slower than you could currently run a fast marathon. See the Magic Mile section for more information. It's best to run the long runs on a stable surface, usually paved. For those who have run a marathon before and want to run faster, see the [TG = __] for recommended distance.

No huffing and puffing! On long runs, you want to be able to carry on a conversation throughout the run—even at the end. A very slow pace, with liberal walk breaks, will allow almost everyone to feel strong on almost every long one. If you're breathing hard at the end of a long one, you need to adjust to a slower pace with more walk breaks from the beginning of the next one.

Don't be afraid to walk. It's okay to walk the entire distance of long runs. If you missed a long run, you can walk gently for the first half of your next long run. When challenged at the end of long runs, just walk the rest of the distance.

Running form: Never sprint during a running segment—keep the feet low to the ground, using a light touch and a relatively short stride. Most runners find that an upright posture is best but use what feels natural for you. Let your foot move in the natural way. Most runners naturally land on the heel and gently roll off the midfoot. Those who try to run in a way that is unnatural increase injury risk.

Walking form: Walk with a gentle stride that is relatively short. Power-walking and walking with a long stride increase injury risk.

Slow down in the heat! Surveys have shown that runners tend to slow down 30 seconds per mile for every 5 degrees above 60 °F (20 sec/km slower for every 2 °C above 14 °C). Please make these pace adjustments on the hot long run days, using more frequent walk breaks to avoid heat stress. Don't wear a hat on hot days, try to run before the sun rises above the horizon, and pour water over the top of your head to keep cool.

Be sure to check the time limit for the race. The Magic Mile, listed next, can give you guidelines as to the expected finish time per mile on the race day. Don't worry if your comfortable long run pace is slower than the pace needed on the race day. On at least one run during the week, practice running at a pace that is 30 seconds per mile (20 sec/km) faster than you need to run in the race to get in before the finish line closes—see the following section on race day practice.

By inserting strategic walk breaks from the beginning of long workouts, you can significantly reduce fatigue. The Run-Walk-Run ratio should correspond to the pace used. Suggested strategies can be found in chapter 12. Two maintenance runs, 30-40 minutes each, will sustain the conditioning needed. Most commonly, these are done on Tuesday and Thursday, but any two days between long runs are okay. Each runner can choose the pace or the Run-Walk-Run ratio for each of these runs. It is suggested that you run on uneven terrain for at least part of these runs.

It is fine to walk the entire distance of a long run if there are challenges.

It is fine to do cross-training on Monday, Wednesday, and Friday, if you wish. There will be little benefit to your running in doing this, but you'll improve overall fitness. On the cross-training days, don't do exercises like stair machines that concentrate effort in the calf muscle.

Standard warm-up: Walk for 3-5 minutes, then, run for a few seconds and walk for one to 5 minutes. Then, gradually increase the amount of running—reducing the amount of walking for 5 minutes—until you reach the ratio that feels comfortable for you.

Run-Walk-Run practice: On Tuesday, after the standard warm-up, try various Run-Walk-Run strategies. For example, if you are currently running a minute/ walking a minute on your long runs, try a few rotations (3-4 min each) of run 30 seconds/walk 30 seconds or 20/20 or 15/15.

Race day practice: On Thursday, after the standard warm-up, time yourself for 2 miles. Use a Run-Walk-Run strategy that feels comfortable. Try to run at a pace that is 30 seconds per mile faster than finish line closing pace if you suspect that this pace might be a challenge on the race day.

Terrain training: Read chapter 15 on terrain training. It is best to devote the middle of one of your short runs each week to this. If you have injuries that could be made worse by uneven terrain, avoid this training until healing occurs. Terrain training can also be done after the Magic Mile on the weekends designated for this or combined with Run-Walk-Run practice or race day practice.

Hill training: After your Magic Mile, on the designated weekends, you can combine terrain training on hilly terrain or alternate hill training one MM weekend and terrain the next.

Standard cool-down: Walk for 10 minutes with a gentle and short stride.

Magic Mile: I suggest doing this after the standard warm-up on the non–long-run weekends listed on the schedule. Over the span of the training you should see steady progress and predict a finish time that is realistic as the race date approaches.
- To convert per mile time into per kilometer time, convert the minutes and seconds into a number with a decimal and then multiply by .62. For example, a 10:00 per mile pace would be 6.2 minutes per kilometer or 6:12 per kilometer.
- This program is the minimum needed to get to the finish. If you want to run more and are not having aches, pains, or other issues, go ahead.
- For veteran marathoners who want to run faster in their trail race, alternative workouts are listed, using [TG = __]. Read chapter 23, Faster Trail Racing, for more information on these workouts and other improvement strategies.

- At www.JeffGalloway.com you can find a timer that will beep or vibrate to tell you when to walk and when to run.

Note: This training advice is given as one runner to another. For medical questions, ask your doctor.

Marathon training schedule

Goal: To finish in the upright position

Who: For runners who have been running for at least six months with no time goal.

Three-day training week:
- Tuesday: 30-40 minutes (including Run-Walk-Run practice and terrain)
- Thursday: 30-40 minutes (including race day practice and terrain)
- Weekend: Listed next

Weekend workouts
[TG = __] is the recommendation for marathon veterans who want to run faster this season.

The schedule:

Week 1: 3-4 miles

Week 2: 4-5 miles

Week 3: 3 miles on trails

Week 4: 5.5 to 6 miles

Week 5: 3 miles on trails

Week 6: 7 miles [TG = 8 mi]

Week 7: 4 miles on trails

Week 8: 9 miles [TG = 10 mi]

Week 9: 4 miles on trails

Week 10: 11 miles [TG = 12 mi]

Week 11: 4 miles on trails

Week 12: 13 miles [TG = 14 mi]

Week 13: 4 miles on trails [TG = 4 x 1 mi]

Week 14: 15 miles [TG = 17 mi]

Week 15: 5 miles on trails [TG = 6 x 1 mi]

Week 16: 17 miles [TG = 20 mi]

Week 17: 5 miles on trails [8 x 1 mi]

Week 18: 6 miles with MM

Week 19: 20 miles [TG = 23 mi]

Week 20: 6 miles on trails [TG 10 x 1 mi]

Week 21: 7 miles with MM

Week 22: 23 miles [TG = 26 mi]

Week 23: 6 miles on trails [TG 12 x 1 mi]

Week 24: 7 miles with MM

Week 25: 26 miles [TG = 29 mi]

Week 26: 6 miles

Week 27: 10 miles on trails [TG = 14 x 1 mi]

Week 28: 7 miles

Week 29: Marathon Race

Week 30: 3 miles

© Thinkstock/iStock

Chapter 22:
Ultra Marathon Training

50K * 50 Mile * 100K * 100 Mile Training Programs

Goal: To finish in the upright position

Who: For runners who have been running for at least 12 months with no time goal. Time goal runners should add one to two miles to each segment on each long weekend.

Note: Veterans who want to run faster need to read chapter 23, Faster Trail Racing.

Welcome to ultra marathon training! This proven training program has led thousands of runners across the finish line, while reducing the chance of injury to almost zero. Only three weekly training days are needed: 30-40 minutes on Tuesday and Thursday and a longer session on the weekend.

The long mileage weekends are the key to ultra marathon training. As you increase the distance of these, you push back your endurance barriers and prepare to go the distance on the race day. You can't go too slowly on the long distance weekends; your goal is simply to finish each one with strength. Generally, you want to slow down at least three minutes per mile slower than you could currently run a fast marathon. See the Magic Mile section for more information. It's best to run the long runs on a stable surface, usually paved. Veterans at the various distances who want to run faster should add one to two miles to each segment throughout the training program for best endurance effect.

No huffing and puffing! On long runs, you want to be able to carry on a conversation throughout the run—even at the end. A very slow pace, with liberal walk breaks, will allow you to feel strong on almost every long one. If you're breathing hard at the end of a long one, you need to adjust to a slower pace with more walk breaks from the beginning of the next one.

Don't be afraid to walk. It's okay to walk the entire distance of long runs. If you missed a long run, you can walk gently for the first half of your next long run. When challenged at the end of long runs, just walk the rest of the distance.

Running form: Never sprint during a running segment—keep the feet low to the ground, using a light touch and a relatively short stride. Most runners find that an upright posture is best but use what feels natural for you. Let your foot move in the natural way. Most runners naturally land on the heel and gently roll off the midfoot. Those who try to run in a way that is unnatural increase injury risk.

Walking form: Walk with a gentle stride that is relatively short. Power-walking and walking with a long stride increase injury risk.

Slow down in the heat! Surveys have shown that runners tend to slow down 30 seconds/mile for every 5 degrees above 60 °F (20 sec/km slower for every 2 °C above 14 °C). Please make these pace adjustments on the hot long run days, using more frequent walk breaks to avoid heat stress. Don't wear a hat on hot days, try to run before the sun rises above the horizon, and pour water over the top of your head to keep cool.

Be sure to check the time limit for the race. The Magic Mile, listed next, can give you guidelines as to the expected finish time, per mile, on the race day. Don't worry if your comfortable long run pace is slower than the pace needed on the race day. On at least one run during the week, practice running at a pace that is 30 seconds/mile (20 sec/km) faster than you need to run in the race to get in before the finish line closes—see the following section on race day practice.

By inserting strategic walk breaks from the beginning of long workouts, you can significantly reduce fatigue. The Run-Walk-Run ratio should correspond to the pace used. Suggested strategies can be found in chapter 12. Two maintenance runs, 30-40 minutes each, will sustain the conditioning needed. Most commonly, these are done on Tuesday and Thursday. Each runner can choose the pace or the Run-Walk-Run ratio for each of these runs. It is suggested that you run on uneven terrain for at least part of these runs.

The long weekends have the distance broken up into segments. Avoid taking more than four hours of rest between segments.

It is fine to walk the entire distance of a segment if there are challenges

It is fine to do cross-training on Monday, Wednesday, and Friday, if you wish. There will be little benefit to your running in doing this, but you'll improve overall fitness. On the cross-training days, don't do exercises like stair machines that concentrate effort in the calf muscle.

Standard warm-up: Walk for 3-5 minutes; then, run for a few seconds and walk for 1 to 5 minutes. Then, gradually increase the amount of running, reducing the amount of walking for 5 minutes—until you reach the ratio that feels comfortable for you.

Run-Walk-Run practice. On Tuesday, after the standard warm-up, try various Run-Walk-Run strategies. For example, if you are currently running a minute/walking a minute, on your long runs, try a few rotations (3-4 min each) of run 30 sec/walk 30 sec or 20/20 or 15/15.

Race day practice: On Thursday, after the standard warm-up, time yourself for two miles. Use a Run-Walk-Run strategy that feels comfortable. Try to run at a pace that is 30 seconds per mile faster than finish line closing pace if you suspect that this pace might be a challenge on the race day.

Terrain training: Read chapter 15 on terrain training. It is best to devote the middle of one of your short runs each week to this. If you have injuries that could be made worse by uneven terrain, avoid this training until healing occurs. Terrain training can also be done after the Magic Mile on the weekends designated for this or combined with Run-Walk-Run practice or race day practice.

Hill training: After your Magic Mile, on the designated weekends, you can combine terrain training on hilly terrain, or alternate hill training one weekend and terrain the next.

Standard cool-down: Walk for 10 minutes with a gentle and short stride.

Magic Mile: I suggest doing this after the standard warm-up on the non-long-run weekends listed on the schedule. Over the span of the training you should see steady progress and predict a finish time that is realistic as the race date approaches.

- To convert per mile time into per kilometer time, convert the minutes and seconds into a number with a decimal and then multiply by .62. For example, a 10:00 per mile pace would be 6.2 minutes per kilometer or 6:12 per kilometer.
- **Note:** At www.JeffGalloway.com you can find a timer that will beep or vibrate to tell you when to walk and when to run.

Note: This training advice is given as one runner to another. For medical questions, ask your doctor.

© Thinkstock/iStock

50 kilometer to 100 mile weekend training schedule

Goal: To finish in the upright position

Strategy:

- Two maintenance runs during the week with a longer one on the weekend
- Every two to four weeks, a series of workouts are done throughout the weekend, as noted next
- Rest between segments: four hours only
- Walk as much as desired; even walking the entire distance will bestow the endurance of the distance
- When tired, walk gently, take extra breaks as needed, and try to complete the distance assigned

Three-day training week:

Tuesday: 30-40 minutes
Thursday: 30-40 minutes
Weekend: Listed next

Note: Prior to starting this program, gradually increase the distance of the weekend workouts to the following (it is okay to walk the entire distance if desired):

For 50 kilometers: 2 miles, 2 miles
For 50 miles: 3 miles, 3 miles
For 100 kilometers: 2 miles, 3 miles, 2 miles
For 100 miles: 3 miles, 4.5 miles, 4.5 miles, 3 miles

Week 1:

For 50 kilometers: 3 miles, 3 miles
For 50 miles: 4.5 miles, 4.5 miles
For 100 kilometers: 3 miles, 4 miles, 3 miles
For 100 miles: 4 miles, 6 miles, 6 miles, 4.5 miles

Week 2:

3 miles

Week 3:

For 50 kilometers: 4 miles, 4 miles

For 50 miles: 6 miles, 6 miles

For 100 kilometers: 4.5 miles, 5.5 miles, 4 miles

For 100 miles: 5 miles, 8 miles, 8 miles, 6 miles

Week 4:

3 miles

Week 5:

For 50 kilometers: 5.5 miles, 5.5 miles

For 50 miles: 8 miles, 8 miles

For 100 kilometers: 6 miles, 7 miles, 5 miles

For 100 miles: 7 miles, 10 miles, 10 miles, 8 miles

Week 6:

4 miles

Week 7:

For 50 kilometers: 7 miles, 7 miles

For 50 miles: 10 miles, 10 miles

For 100 kilometers: 8 miles, 9 miles, 7 miles

For 100 miles: 9 miles, 12 miles, 12 miles, 10 miles

Week 8:

4 miles

Week 9:

For 50 kilometers: 9 miles, 9 miles

For 50 miles: 12 miles, 12 miles

For 100 kilometers: 10 miles, 11 miles, 9 miles

For 100 miles: 12 miles, 15 miles, 15 miles, 13 miles

Week 10:

4 miles

Week 11:

5 miles

Week 12:

For 50 kilometers: 10 miles, 10 miles

For 50 miles: 11 miles, 10 miles, 6 miles

For 100 kilometers: 12 miles, 13 miles, 11 miles

For 100 miles: 15 miles, 17 miles, 18 miles, 15 miles

Week 13:

4 miles

Week 14:

5 miles

Week 15:

For 50 kilometers: 12 miles, 12 miles

For 50 miles: 12 miles, 12 miles, 8 miles

For 100 kilometers: 12 miles, 15 miles, 13 miles

For 100 miles: 15-18 miles, 19 miles, 21 miles, 18 miles

Week 16:

5 miles

Week 17:

6 miles

Week 18:

For 50 kilometers: 14 miles, 12 miles

For 50 miles: 14 miles, 12 miles, 10 miles

For 100 kilometers: 14 miles, 17 miles, 15 miles

For 100 miles: 17-20 miles, 21 miles, 24 miles, 20 miles

Week 19:

5 miles

Week 20:

8 miles

Week 21:

6 miles with MM

Week 22:

For 50 kilometers: 16 miles, 14 miles

For 50 miles: 16 miles, 14 miles, 12 miles

For 100 kilometers: 16 miles, 19 miles, 17 miles

For 100 miles: 17-20 miles, 21 miles, 24 miles, 20 miles

Week 23:

6 miles

Week 24:

9 miles

Week 25:

6 miles

Week 26:

For 50 kilometers: 18 miles, 16 miles

For 50 miles: 18 miles, 16 miles, 14 miles

For 100 kilometers: 18 miles, 21 miles, 19 miles

For 100 miles: 18-22 miles, 23 miles, 26 miles, 21 miles

Week 27:

6 miles

Week 28:

9 miles with MM

Week 29:

7 miles

Week 30:

Race weekend

Week 31:

3 miles—Relax, you've earned it!

Chapter 23:
Faster Trail Racing

Running faster on trail courses is accomplished primarily by being stronger to the end of the race. Longer distance weekends and the appropriate speedwork can raise your fitness to a higher level. Pacing conservatively is the other major component. This will allow you to be stronger to the end of the race, avoiding the exhaustion "wall" with a dramatic slowdown during the last third of the race.

But there are many challenges on a trail that are beyond your control and can slow you down. Temperatures above 60 °F are the most significant. Be sure to read the segment in this book about heat issues and slow down as the temperature rises, even if you have a time goal. Failure to do so can result in heat stroke and even death. I'm against death.

Note: First timers in any event should not try for a time goal. After you have run one event at that distance, you can shift into a time goal schedule.

To run as fast as the weather and the course allow, there are a series of training elements that I recommend: speed training, longer long runs, form drills, race pace segments, hill training, and the right Run-Walk-Run strategy.

Strategy can make a huge difference in your performance. Just as you must raise your physiological limits by speed training and your endurance through long runs, a well-organized training plan can give you the confidence and a strategy to keep going when others back off.

Schedules for running faster are basically the same as the schedules for those who just want to finish. The time goal weekend workouts are listed on the schedule of the 5K, 10K, half, and marathon programs in the previous chapters. When you see, [TG =], you are working out for a time goal. The long run distance needs to be longer by a few miles on each, and the additional miles are the listed TG. For the longer events, add one to two miles to each segment—walking this additional distance is fine.

© Brennan Galloway

For the ultra events (50K, 50 mile, 100K, 100 mile), I don't include speedwork but recommend that you enter some half marathons and marathons during the first three months of your program as part of your long segment weekends. It helps to run one segment before the race and then run the race as a hard training run—but not all-out. During the second half of the program, a half marathon could be scheduled one or two weeks after each long weekend.

Course preview: Even if you hike the course in segments, going over each mile will give you the knowledge to structure training and to set your strategy for running the race. Make notes as to where you should back off, walk, and walk around a rough area. Your feet can start to adapt to the surface. Mind and spirit will know when you are getting closer to the end. Many trail racers have told me that hiking at least the last half of the course was crucial in their strategy, confidence, and success.

Race strategy: After a thorough preview, you can plan your training to prepare for the various portions of the course. Hill work can be done one day per week, using hills that are similar to the ones on the course. Spend significant time training on the type of terrain where you can do the best in the race. But also schedule a few workouts to help improve on weak areas.

Trial races: Run a few trail races on similar terrain as your race course but at shorter distances than your goal race. Run at the pace you want to run in your goal race, trying various strategies and Run-Walk-Run ratios until you feel confident in what you'll use in the race itself.

Longer long runs: Going beyond goal race distance in a slow long run has been a proven way of sustaining muscle performance and mental confidence at the end of a race. This can result in a significant time improvement. See the training schedules for recommended distances.

Speedwork: This is listed on the marathon and half marathon schedule. This should be run on a stable surface and not on rough terrain. A track, road, or paved trail are the best venues.

Long runs: Run at least three minutes per mile slower than you are currently running in the marathon (or the Magic Mile predicts you can run in a fast marathon).

Marathon: The mile repeats for a faster marathon should be run 30-45 seconds per mile faster than goal race pace. Walk five minutes between each. Use a variety of Run-Walk-Run strategies to see which works best for you at that pace.

Half marathon: The half mile repetitions for a faster half marathon should be run 15-20 seconds faster than goal race pace per half mile. Walk three minutes between each. Try various Run-Walk-Run strategies to see which works best at that pace.

Terrain training: Run carefully on the various types of uneven terrain so you can develop better technique and strategies for the race itself. Read chapter 15 on terrain training.

Recovery: You should not run the day after uneven terrain workouts or complete only very stable and easy runs. It's best to take a day or two off from exercise before the long workout days. After long runs and speed sessions, take a day off from any exercise that uses the calf muscles.

Time goal program

Tuesday 30-45 min: Run-walk-un easily for half a mile. Then do 4-8 cadence drills. Then do 4-8 acceleration-gliders. Then do terrain training as noted in chapter 15.

Thursday 30-45 min: Run-Walk-Run easily for half a mile. Then do 4-8 cadence drills. Then do 4-8 acceleration-gliders. Then do hill training as noted in chapter 16.

Weekend: Follow the weekend plan in this book based upon the distance of your goal race. Time goal workouts are listed as [TG =].

Chapter 24:
Strategy and Plans for Trail Runs

Each trail run is an adventure. The best approach is to be prepared for almost anything. If you are entering a race or are running on a trail that is used in a race, do a computer search for the runner reviews of the race course by past participants. These can be very honest and identify the major challenges. Read over chapter 10 on equipment and always bring a cell phone unless there is no reception in the trail area.

Take a tour of the course: Whether you run the course at one time or in segments, it really helps to hike or run the course in advance. You'll get to know what the terrain is like, when to expect the hills, how steep they are, what are the obstacles, and hopefully how to keep from getting lost. During very long trail runs, it is wonderful to be able to recognize the last few miles of the course, landmarks, and correct trails.

Make your own map of the course: You can use an existing map or make your own. Make notes about the hills and how difficult the course is. Highlight the uneven surface areas. Mark the location of water hazards, creeks, and natural drainage areas in case of rain or runoff. Note the downhills and if the surface is unstable due to sand, rocks, or water on a rock face.

Designate the trail intersections: The first time you run on a trail (and every time for those who tend to get lost), spend a few minutes to understand which path to take. Make notes about how to tell you are going the right way by noting landmarks after trail intersections to verify that you are on the right path. Carry some bright flagging tape or some other marking agent to chart your way back if you need to do so.
Uphills: A high percentage of trail runners walk all or most of the uphill segments. This saves resources, especially early in the race.

Downhills: Most of the trail runners I've coached have had more trouble running downhill than up. Unstable surface poses the greatest danger due to falls at unusual angles. Top priority is to maintain secure footing even if you have to walk part or all of the downhill. Once you feel that the surface is secure you can adapt the downhill running technique provided next so that it works for you.

Pacing: It's always better to be conservative and run slower in the beginning, with more walking. GPS and accelerometer devices will help you track the distance. It also helps to have a separate stop watch to track your running time.

Water placement: Some courses allow you to stash water in advance. If this is not possible, carry water with you in a Fitletic belt, camelback, or equipment of your choice. Suggested intake is two to four ounces every two miles.

Support: Some races allow for runners to have a support team to bring water, help with directions, and provide back-up flashlights and batteries, etc. Some

races allow you to drop off special foods the day before, which will be taken to the aid stations on the course.

Weather options: Be sure to read chapter 8 on clothing and pay particular attention to the clothing thermometer table. Visit a weather site, such as weather.com, before you start the run and line up the clothing you might need.

The last few miles: If you can only preview one section of the course, make it the last three to five miles. Schedule your travel so you arrive an extra day or two early and hike the final segment. Make notes to yourself as to when you could start picking up the pace if you feel good. Since your legs will be fatigued and not as stable, identify sections of the trail that could be hazardous. Many of the runners I've trained have missed key turns at the end of the race due to mental fatigue.

© Thinkstock/iStock

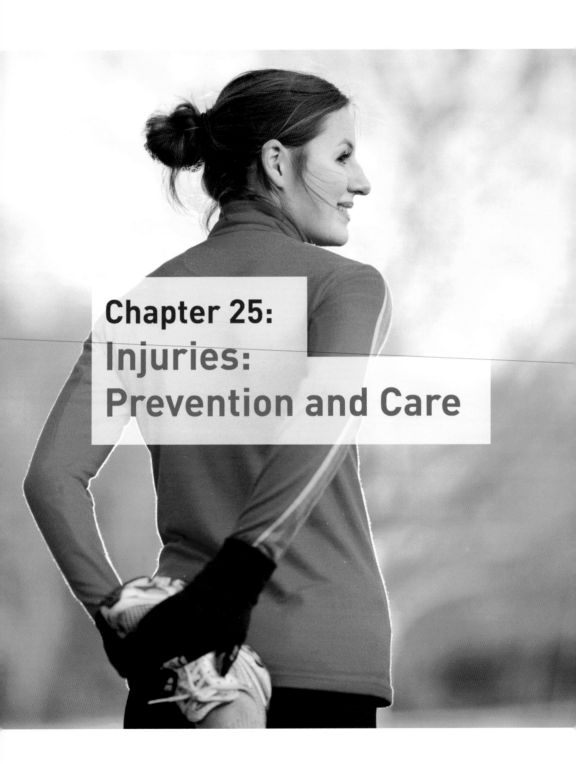

Chapter 25:
Injuries:
Prevention and Care

Why do micro-tears accumulate?

- Constant use (insufficient rest between stress workouts)
- Uneven terrain; failure to walk through rough terrain
- Prior damage
- Speedwork
- Too many races
- Doing something different
- Sudden increase of workload
- Not enough walk breaks during long runs
- Stretching can actually cause many injuries

Common causes of injuries

It's a physiological fact that the constant use of a muscle, tendon, or joint, without a break, will result in earlier fatigue and reduced work potential. Continuing to run or walk when the muscle is extremely fatigued increases the quantity of micro-tears dramatically and is a major cause of injury.

Pacing conservatively and inserting walk breaks early and often in long runs and stressful workouts will gain each runner a great deal of control over the fatigue process, while allowing muscles, tendons, feet, and joints to repair damage and maintain capacity. This lowers the chance of breakdown by significantly reducing the accumulating damage that leads to injury.

Note: This information is given as one runner to another and not meant to be medical advice. See a doctor for medical issues.

Tools that can give you control over your aches and pains:

- Be sensitive to weak links, and let aggravations heal by strategic rest and treatment immediately when you experience a potential injury.

- Run long runs at least three minutes per mile slower than current marathon race pace (or from Magic Mile computation for a fast marathon).
- Take all walk breaks recommended on long runs based upon pace per mile.
- Avoid stretching weak links; stretching worsens or causes many injuries.
- Don't try to change your running form significantly.
- Shoes: Get professional fitting advice from the experts in a good running store.
- Gradually break in a new shoe; don't shift suddenly from a worn shoe to a new one.
- Run on stable terrain (e.g., track, road, or bike trail). Do your terrain training in small doses.

Speedwork issues:

- ~~Don't do speedwork if you don't have a time goal.~~
- Speedwork segments are paced according to the recommendations in this book.
- Run speedwork and long runs at the right pace for YOU and not that of faster runners.
- Gradually increase the speed and distance of workouts—no sudden increases.
- Take the full rest interval between speed segments recommended in this book.
- Run speedwork on a track or a paved surface.

Aggravating factors:

- Prior damage, especially due to accident trauma, football, soccer, or skiing. It may not be possible for all of the damage to be repaired. In most cases, training adjustments can be made.
- Shoes are too worn.
- Terrain is too rough.
- Speed training and frequent racing increases stress on the weak links significantly. I have found individual training adjustments can often allow

for continued training, but sometimes there needs to be a "vacation from speed" for a week or two.

- Stride length: Longer strides increase risk. A shorter stride may not slow you down if you will increase cadence or turnover. (See the section on the cadence drills.)
- Bounce off the ground: the higher the bounce, the more stress on feet, legs, and joints. The higher the bounce, the more shock to be absorbed upon landing. Stay low to the ground, touching lightly.
- Stretching: I have heard from thousands of runners who have been injured or had injuries worsened by stretching. In general, I do not recommend stretching. There are individuals who benefit from certain stretches, however. Be careful if you choose to stretch. Stretching is not generally found to be beneficial as a warm-up or cool-down activity and causes injuries when done at these times. Trying to "stretch out" fatigue-induced tightness often results in injury and prolonged recovery.
- **Note:** Those who have iliotibial band injury can often get relief from a few specific stretches that act as a quick fix to keep you running. Even when doing these, be careful. The foam roller treatment has been the mode that has reduced healing time for this injury. There is a picture on our website (www.JeffGalloway.com) that shows you how to use this.
- Continuing to work out when an injury has begun can dramatically increase the damage in a few minutes. It is always better to stop the exercise immediately if there is an indication that you have an injury and take two to three days off from running to get the healing started.
- Avoid certain exercises that worsen your weak links (different for the individual).
- The Toe Squincher: I recommend that all runners do this exercise every day to reduce and eliminate the chance of having a plantar fascia injury—or other foot problems. Point your foot down and contract the muscles in the forefoot/midfoot region. This strengthens the many little muscles in your feet that will provide extra support.

Note: Studies show that runners have healthier joints and fewer orthopedic complaints than non-runners.

How do you know if you are injured?

Continuing to exercise when you feel that you might have an injury puts you at great risk for an extended pause from running. In most cases that I've monitored, when I suspect that there is an injury, it usually is an injury. Be sensitive to your weak links. When you notice any of the following symptoms, take at least a day or two off from running.

- **Inflammation:** Look for swelling, puffiness, or thickening.
- **Loss of function:** The area doesn't work correctly or move normally.
- **Pain:** If the pain does not go away as you get warmed up and walk slowly, or the pain increases, STOP!

You can take up to five days off from running with no significant loss in conditioning.

It is always better to err on the conservative side of injury repair. If you take an extra day off at the beginning of an injury you won't lose any conditioning. But if you continue training with an injury, you may increase the healing time by a week or a month for each day you try to push through pain.

Quick action can reduce recovery time needed.

Some minor irritation may require just one day off from running. As the pain level increases, so does the need for more recovery days.

How to train while injured (if injury allows):

- Get the okay from a doctor to continue training (find a doctor who wants you to run when you can).
- Stay below the threshold of further irritation.
- Work out every other day.

- Insert walk breaks and shuffle breaks into runs.
- Avoid faster running or gently ease back into faster running.
- Don't stretch (unless you have certain stretches that work for you and don't hurt you).
- Long run endurance can often be maintained by walking the distance of the long one when injured.

How to reduce the risk of speed injuries:

- Warm-up: Start very slowly, gradually accelerate, and ease into the workout.
- Run the first and the last repetition more slowly than the others. Don't race the last repetition.
- Rest between repetitions. When you have a history of speed injuries, take more rest.
- Some runners are more prone to injury than others. It is better to take an extra day or two off if you sense the healing is not adequate for running.
- If you already have a weak link irritation, don't do a speed workout or any workout that could make it worse.

How to stay in shape when injured:

- Many running injuries will heal while you continue to run, if you stay below the threshold of further irritation. Talk to your doctor about this issue to ensure that the healing has started and that you are not irritating the injury as you start back. Most injuries allow for walking the distance of the long runs. This will provide all of the endurance as from running the long run.
- Cross-training: Pick an activity that does not worsen the injury. Water running is the best for maintaining running conditioning. To hold current endurance, schedule a long water-run session that is the same number of water-running minutes you would spend running your current long run. Some runners have been able to maintain speed conditioning by doing a speed-running workout in the water once a week.

- Swimming and cycling are good for overall fitness but don't have a lot of direct benefit to runners.
- Activities to avoid: Anything that irritates the injury.
- If you can walk, walk for at least an hour every other day.

How to return to running:

- Check with your doctor to ensure that enough healing has occurred to begin running again.
- Stay below the threshold of irritation. You want to see progress, week by week, in reduction of pain.
- Stay in touch with your doctor and ask questions if you suspect that you are making the injury worse.
- Avoid exercising if you are favoring the injured area or limping. Running in an abnormal way can result in an even worse injury in another part your body.
- If you haven't been running, start by walking. Build up to a 30-minute walk.
- Insert small segments of running into a walk (run 5-10 seconds, walk the rest of the minute). If there is no aggravation, you could increase five seconds on the running segment while decreasing five seconds on the walking segment—after using each new ratio for at least two workouts.
- Avoid anything that could further injure the problem area.
- First increase the duration of the long run by 5-10 minutes every other week. Keep the Run-Walk-Run ratio mostly walking for the first week before increasing.

Injuries caused by running form mistakes

While the body adapts and adjusts to the running motion, workouts or races that are long and strenuous can result in irregularities in our normal form. Since the body is not adapted to these "wobbles," weak links can be irritated. Continued use and using an unaccustomed range of motion can lead to injury. Following are some of the common ones. For more information, see my book *Running Injuries: Treatment and Prevention* and a knowledgeable sports medicine doctor.

Troubleshooting form-related injuries

- Lower back: Caused by forward lean, over-stride, or too few walk breaks.
- Neck pain: Caused by forward lean or head placed too far forward or back.
- Hamstring pain: Caused by striding too long or stretching.
- Shin pain on front: Caused by too long of a stride length, especially on downhills or at end of run.
- Shin pain on inside: Caused by over pronation or uneven terrain.
- Achilles: Caused by stretching, speedwork, or over-pronating.
- Calf pain: Caused by stretching, speedwork, or inadequate number of walk breaks on long runs.
- Knee pain: Caused by too few walk breaks, over-pronation, speedwork, or extended stride.

The shuffle

The most efficient and gentle running form is a shuffle: The feet stay next to the ground, touching lightly with a relatively short stride. When running at the most relaxed range of the shuffling motion, the ankle mechanism does a great deal of the work and little effort is required from the calf muscle. But when the foot pushes harder and bounces more and the stride increases, there are often more aches, pains, and injuries.

Speedwork increases injury risk.

Time goal runners need to run faster in some workouts. This means some increase in stride length, greater bounce, and foot pushing. By gradually increasing the intensity of speed training (with sufficient rest intervals and rest days between), feet and legs can adapt. But there is still a risk of injury. Be sensitive to your weak links and don't keep running if there is the chance that you may have the beginnings of an injury.

Correct posture can reduce aches and pains.

Posture is an individual issue. Most of the runners I've worked with find that an upright posture (like a puppet on a string) is best in all ways. When runners use a forward lean, there is a tendency to develop lower back and neck pain. A small minority of runners run with a forward lean with no problems. In this case, one should run the way that is most natural to the runner.

Suggestions for running smoother and reducing irritation to weak links:

- **Feet:** They should be low to the ground, using a light touch of the foot.
- Try not to bounce more than an inch off the ground.
- Let your feet move the way that is natural for them. If you tend to land on your heel and roll forward, do so.
- If you have motion control issues, a foot device can provide minor correction to bring you into alignment and avoid irritating a weak link. A supportive shoe is also needed.
- **Legs:** Maintain a gentle stride that allows your leg muscles to stay relaxed. In general, it's better to have a shorter stride and focus on quicker turnover if you want to speed up.
- Water-running can help in reducing flips and turns of the feet and legs, which sometimes cause injuries, aches, and pains. Using a flotation device, run in the deep end of a pool so your feet do not touch the bottom. Even one session of 15 minutes, once a week, can be beneficial.

Cramps in the muscles?

At some point, most people who take long trail runs will experience at least an occasional cramp. These muscle contractions usually occur in the feet or the calf muscles and may come during a run or walk, or they may hit at random afterward. Very commonly, they will occur at night when you are sitting around at your desk or watching TV. When severe cramps occur during a run, you will have to stop or slow down significantly.

The most common cause of muscle cramping is overexerting the muscle, especially during the first mile or so. A slower warm-up often helps, as does a slower pace at the beginning of a workout. Running too hard on hilly terrain is also a cause. Medications, especially statin drugs, often cause cramping during exercise. If this is a possible cause, talk to your doctor; there may be a medication that allows you to run cramp-free. An over-the-counter salt tablet called Succeed! has been very effective in reducing cramping when it was related to sodium depletion. Cramping is common in the very long, long weekends and ultra marathon races.

Cramps vary in severity. Most are mild, but some can grab so hard that they shut down the muscles and hurt when they seize up. Light massage can relax the muscle and allow it to get back to work. Stretching usually increases the damage from the cramp, tearing the muscle fibers, according to my experience.

Most cramps are due to overuse—doing more than in the recent past or continuing to put yourself at your limit, especially in warm weather. Look at the pace and distance of your runs and workouts in your training journal to see if you have been running too far, too fast, or both. Remember to adjust long run pace for heat: 20-30 seconds a mile slower for each 5 °F of temperature increase above 60 °F—or, respectively, 20 seconds/kilometer slower for every 2 °C of temperature increase above 14 °C.

- Continuous running increases cramping. Taking walk breaks more often can reduce or eliminate them. Numerous runners who used to cramp on long runs when they ran continuously stopped cramping when they increased the frequency of the walks and decreased the length of the run segment.
- During hot weather, a good electrolyte beverage (consumed during the day, during the 24 hours after a long or hard run and during the four-hour rest periods on long weekends) can help to replace the fluids and electrolytes that your body loses in sweating. Accelerade has been the most effective drink in my experience. Drink about six to eight ounces every two to four hours throughout the day.

Here are several ways of dealing with cramps:

- Take a longer and more gentle warm-up.
- Shorten your run segment or take walk breaks more often.
- Slow down your walk and walk more.
- Take a longer warm-up during speed sessions.
- Look at any other exercise that could be causing the cramps.
- Take a buffered salt tablet during your long workouts (follow the directions on the label).
- Don't push off as hard or bounce as high off the ground.
- Shorten your stride length.
- During speed workouts on hot days, walk more during the rest interval.
- Walk up hills.

Exercises that can prevent and treat injuries

Plantar fascia and foot injuries: The toe squincher
This strengthens the many muscles in the foot, promoting a strong push-off, reducing foot fatigue, and reducing foot damage. Point your foot down and contract the muscles of the foot, which will cause the toes to curl in. Keep the contraction until the foot cramps. This can be done when wearing shoes or not, 15-20 times a day.

Back and shoulder soreness and pain: Arm running/the crunch
Holding dumbbells (hand-held weights) in each hand, go through a slightly exaggerated motion you would use when running for a set of 10 reps (one left and one right equals one repetition). Pick a weight that is heavy enough so that you feel you have strengthened the shoulder and neck muscles, but not so much that you struggle to finish the last two repetitions.

Iliotibial band: Foam roller

This is the best treatment I've found for speeding the healing of the IT band. Use a cylinder of dense foam (illustrated on www.JeffGalloway.com). Lie down on your side, where the IT pain is felt. Rest your bodyweight on the roller and move your body (pressing down on the roller) with your hands so that you're rolling from below the pain site to just above it. Roll for five minutes before the run, five minutes after the run, and five minutes before bed at night (probably the most effective).

Ice massage for achilles and other tendons next to the skin

Freeze a paper cup or Styrofoam cup of water. Peel off the outer layer at the top so it's just a chunk of ice. Rub the ice constantly over the tendon for 15 minutes. The area should be numb after the treatment.

Night treatments may help more than others.

Experts tell me that most of the healing occurs overnight. If you perform one of these treatments before you go to bed, you may speed up the healing process.

If you are sensitive to your weak links, take the appropriate walk breaks and rest days, stop training when there could be an injury, and treat a damaged body part, you may avoid all serious injuries. This will bestow the greatest reward from running: enjoyment of every run.

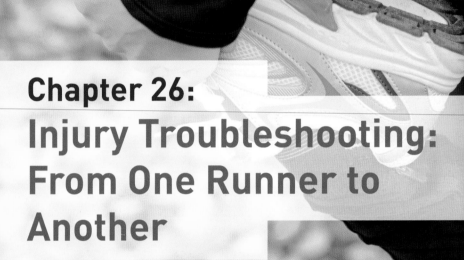

Chapter 26:
Injury Troubleshooting: From One Runner to Another

Note: As with all medical issues, ask a doctor who wants you to continue running.

Trail running increases the risk of foot and ankle injuries. By shortening your stride and walking through areas of rough terrain, you will reduce the risks. The reality is that most trail runners experience some irritation during a season. Here are the more common injuries that my runners deal with and their solutions.

© Thinkstock/iStock

Quick treatment tips

For all injuries:

1. Take three to five days off from running.
2. Avoid any activity that could worsen the injury.
3. As you return to running, stay below the threshold of further irritation with much more liberal walking.
4. Don't stretch unless you have iliotibial-band injury. Stretching interferes with the healing of most injuries that I've worked with.
5. As you start to run again, use short segments of running or more walking.
6. For the first two to three weeks after returning to running, avoid rough terrain.

Muscle injuries:

1. Ask your doctor if you can take prescription strength anti-inflammatory medication. Always follow your doctor's advice about medication.
2. See a sports massage therapist who has worked successfully on many runners.

Tendon and foot injuries:

1. Rub a chunk of ice directly on the area for 15 minutes every night (keep rubbing until the area gets numb).
   Note: Ice bags, or gel ice don't seem to do any good at all.
2. Foot injuries sometimes are helped by an air cast at first to let the foot or leg to be stabilized so that the healing can begin.

Knee injuries:

1. Ask your doctor if you can take prescription strength anti-inflammatory medication.
2. See if you can do a little gentle walking; sometimes this helps.
3. Sometimes the knee straps can relieve pain; ask your doctor.
4. Get a shoe-check to see if you are in the right shoe (if you overpronate, a motion control shoe may help).
5. If you over pronate, an orthotic may help.
6. If you have internal knee pain, glucosamine supplement, may help.
7. Take more frequent walk breaks.

Running before the injury has completely healed

With most running injuries, you can continue to run even while the injury is healing. Always check with a doctor to be sure. First, you must have some time off to get the healing started. If you do this at the beginning of an injury, you may only need two to five days off. The longer you try to push through the problem, the more damage you produce and the longer it will take to heal. Stay in touch with the doctor at any stage of this healing–running process, follow your doctor's advice, and use your best judgment.

To allow for healing once you have returned to running, stay below the threshold of further irritation. In other words, if the injury feels a little irritated when running at 2.5 miles and starts hurting a little at 3 miles, you should run no more than 2 miles. And if your healthy run-walk ratio is 3 minutes run/1 minute walk, you should drop back to 1:1 or 30 seconds/30 seconds.

Always allow a rest day between running days. With most injuries you can cross train to maintain conditioning, but make sure that your injury will allow this. Again, your doctor can advise.

Best cross-training modes to maintain your running conditioning

Before doing any of these talk to your doctor. Most are fine for most injuries. But some increase the risk of irritating the injured area and delaying the healing process. For more information on this, see *Running Injuries: Treatment and Prevention* (Hannaford/Galloway). Gradually build up the cross-training, because you have to condition those muscles gradually as you train the running muscles. Even walking is a great way to maintain conditioning if the injury and the doctor will allow it.

1. Run in water to help improve your running form.
2. Use Nordic Track machines.
3. Walk.
4. Use rowing machines.
5. Use elliptical machines.

Treatment suggestions—From one runner to another

Knee pain

Most knee problems will go away if you stop running immediately (don't run the last mile) and take five days off. Ask your doctor if you can use anti-inflammatory medication. Try to figure out what caused the knee problem. Make sure that your running courses don't have a slant or canter. Look at the most worn pair of shoes you have—even walking shoes. If there is wear on the inside of the forefoot, you probably over-pronate. If you have repeat issues with knee pain, you may need a foot support or orthotic. If there is pain under the kneecap, or arthritis, the glucosamine and chondroitin products have helped. The best I've found in this category is the Joint Maintenance supplement by Cooper Complete.

Outside of the knee pain—Iliotibial band syndrome

This band of fascia acts as a tendon, going down the outside of the leg from the hip to just below the knee. The pain is most commonly noticed on the outside of the knee but can occur anywhere along the IT band. I believe this to be a "wobble injury." When the running muscles get tired, they don't keep you on a straight running track. The IT band tries to restrain the wobbling motion, but it cannot and gets overused. Most of the feedback I receive from runners and doctors is that once the healing has started (usually a few days off from running), most runners will heal as fast when you run on it as from a complete stop. In this case, however it is crucial to get your doctor's okay to run and then stay below the threshold of further irritation.

Treatment for Iliotibial Band Syndrome:
- **Stretching:** Stretching the IT band releases the tightness that causes the pain. With this injury you can stretch it at the first sign that it is getting tighter during a run.

- **Self-massage using a foam roller:** This device has helped thousands of runners get over IT band syndrome. On www.RunInjuryFree.com is a picture of someone using a foam roller. Put the roller on the floor, lie on it using bodyweight to press and roll the area that is sore. Rolling before a run will help it warm up, and rolling afterward often helps the injury recover faster. To speed up healing, roll it for five minutes before bed.
- **Massage therapy:** An experienced and accomplished massage therapist can tell whether massage will help and where to massage. The two areas for possible attention are the connecting points of the connective tissue that is tight and the fascia band itself in several places. The stick is a self-massage roller device that has also helped many runners recover from IT band syndrome as they run. As with the foam roller, it helps to warm up the area before a run and to roll it out afterward.
- **Walking is generally fine:** Usually you can find a run-walk ratio that works. Maintain a short stride.
- **Ice massage:** Directly massage the pain air, completing 15 minutes of continuous rubbing every night.

Shin pain: Shin splints or stress fractures

Almost always, pain in the shin indicates a minor irritation called shin splints that allows running and walking as you heal. With normal shin splints, the greatest pain or irritation during injury is during the first mile of a run. Usually the pain gradually goes away as you run and walk. It takes a while to fully heal, so you must have patience.

Inside pain: posterior shin splints. Irritation of the inside of the leg, coming up from the ankle, is called *posterior tibial shin splints* and is often due to over-pronation of the foot (foot rolls in at push-off).

Front of shin: anterior shin splints. When the pain is in the muscle on the front of the lower leg, it is called *anterior tibial shin splints*. This is very often due to having too long a stride when running and especially when walking. Downhill terrain should be avoided as much as possible during the healing process.

Stress fracture: If the pain is in a very specific place and increases as you run, you could have a more serious problem—a stress fracture. This is unusual for beginning runners but characteristic of those who do too much, too soon. It can also indicate low bone density. If you even suspect a stress fracture, do not run or do anything stressful on the leg and see a doctor. Stress fractures take weeks of no running and walking, usually wearing a cast. They may also indicate a calcium deficiency.

Heel pain: Plantar fasciitis
The most effective treatment is putting your foot in a supportive shoe before your first step in the morning.

This very common injury (pain on the inside or center of the heel) is felt when you first walk on the foot in the morning. As you get warmed up, it gradually goes away, only to return the next morning. The most important treatment is to put your foot in a supportive shoe before you step out of bed. Be sure to get a shoe check at a technical running store to make sure that you have the right shoe for your foot. If the pain continues during the day, you should consult with a podiatrist. Usually the doctor will construct a foot support that will surround your arch and heel. This does not always need to be a hard orthotic and is usually a softer one designed for your foot with support in the right places.

The Toe Squincher exercise can help develop foot strength that will also support the foot. It takes several weeks for this to take effect. This is another injury that usually allows for running as you heal, but stay in touch with your doctor. Be sure to avoid fast running and uneven terrain.

Back of the foot: Achilles tendon
The Achilles tendon is the narrow band of tendon rising up from the heel and connecting to the calf muscle. It is part of a very efficient mechanical system, which performs like a strong rubber band to leverage a lot of work out of the foot with little effort from the calf muscle. It is usually injured due to excessive stretching, either through running or through stretching exercises. First, avoid

any activity that stretches the tendon in any way. It helps to add a small heel lift to all shoes, which reduces the range of motion. Every night, rub a chunk of ice directly on the tendon. Keep rubbing for about 15 minutes, until the tendon gets numb. Bags of ice or frozen gels don't do any good at all, in my opinion. Usually after three to five days off from running, the icing takes hold and the tendon feels stronger each day. Anti-inflammatory medication very rarely helps with the Achilles tendon irritation, in my experience.

Hip and groin pain

There are a variety of elements that could be worsened in the hip area. Since the hips are not designed to move you down the road, they are usually abused when you continue to push on and when the calf muscle is too tired to keep you going at top capacity. Ask your doctor about prescription strength anti-inflammatory medication, as this can sometimes speed up recovery. Avoid stretching and any activity that irritates the area.

Calf muscle

The calf is the most important muscle for running. It is often irritated by speedwork and can be pushed into injury by stretching, running too fast when tired, too many speed sessions without adequate rest between, and sprinting at the end of races or workouts.

Deep tissue massage has been the best treatment for most calf muscle problems. Try to find a very experienced massage therapist who has helped lots of runners with calf problems. This can be painful but may be the only way to remove some bio-damage in the muscle. The stick roller can be very beneficial in manipulating tissue out of the area of damage and promoting blood flow (see our website for more information on this product).

Don't stretch! Stretching will tear the muscle fibers that are trying to heal. Avoid running hills and take very frequent walk breaks as you return to running. A slight heel lift (felt) can take pressure off the Achilles to reduce aggravation. As the pain goes away, remove the heel pad.

Chapter 27: Respect the Heat!

© Thinkstock/iStock

When you exercise strenuously in even moderate heat (above 60 °F [14 °C]), you raise core body temperature. Most beginning runners will feel the internal temperature rise above 55 °F (12 °C). This triggers a release of blood into the capillaries of your skin to help cool you down. But this diversion reduces the blood supply available to your exercising muscles, meaning that you will have less blood and less oxygen delivered to the power source that moves you forward and less blood to move out the waste products. As the waste builds up in the muscle, you will slow down.

The bad news is that in warm weather you are going to feel worse and run slower. The worse news is that working too hard on a hot day could result in a very serious condition called heat disease. Make sure that you read the section on this health problem at the end of this chapter. The good news is that you can adapt to these conditions to some extent, as you learn the best time of the day, clothing, and other tricks to keep you cool. But it is always better to back off or stop running at the first sign that you or one of your teammates may be coming into this condition. The following are proven ways of avoiding heat adversity.

Running the long trail workouts during summer heat

1. Run before the sun gets above the horizon. Get up early during the warm months and you will avoid most of the dramatic stress from the sun. This is particularly a problem in humid areas. Also, early morning is usually the coolest time of the day. Without having to deal with the sun, most runners can gradually adapt to heat. At the very least, your runs will be more enjoyable than later in the day. Note: Be sure to take care of safety issues. You may have to wait until there is adequate light to see trail challenges. In southern areas, there are more snakes in the early morning hours, for example.

2. If you must run when the sun is up, pick a shady course. Shade provides a significant relief in areas of low humidity, as well as some relief in humid environments.

3. In areas of low humidity, it's usually cool during the evening and night. In humid environments there may not be much relief. The coolest time of the day when it's humid is just before dawn.

4. Use a pool for some short runs. Water running can be a replacement for a short and easy run.

5. Use treadmills during preseason short run days. Some runners alternate segments on hot days: 5-10 minutes outdoors and 5-10 minutes indoors.

6. Don't wear a hat! You lose most of your body heat through the top of your head. Covering the head will cause a quicker internal build-up of heat.

7. Wear light clothing, but not cotton. Many of the new, technical fibers (polypro, coolmax, drifit) will move moisture away from your skin, producing a cooling effect. Cotton soaks up the sweat, making the garment heavier as it sticks to your skin. This means that you won't receive as much of a cooling effect as that provided by the high-tech products.

8. Pour water over your head. Evaporation not only helps the cooling process, it makes you feel cooler. This psychological boost can be huge. If you can bring along ice water with you, you will feel a lot cooler as you squirt some regularly over the top of your head, using a pop-top water bottle.

9. Do your runs in installments.
   Short runs: It is fine on a hot day that is scheduled for an easy run to put in your 30 minutes by doing 10 in the morning, 10 at noon, and 10 at night.
   Speed sessions: More rest can be taken between speed reps, and you may break up the distance when it's hot (running twice as many 400s if you were scheduled for 800-meter repeats).
   Long runs: You can take a 5-minute cold shower break every 20-30 minutes during a long run. Some runners take a 5-minute soak in the pool.
   Ultra marathon long weekends: You can take four hours between segments.

10. Sun screen: a mixed review. Some runners will need to protect themselves. Some products, however, produce a coating on the skin, reducing the cooling effect of perspiration and resulting in a body temperature build-up. If you are only in the sun for 30-50 minutes at a time, you may not need to put on sunscreen for cancer protection. Consult with your doctor about your specific needs or find a product that doesn't block the pores.

11. Drink six to eight ounces of a sports drink, such as Accelerade, or water at least every two hours or when thirsty throughout the day during hot weather (not when running) and on the four-hour rest between running segments on long run weekend.

12. Look at the clothing thermometer in this book and at www.JeffGalloway. com. Wear loose-fitting garments that have some texture in the fabric. Texture will limit or prevent the perspiration from clinging and sticking to the skin.

13. When the temperature is above 90 °F, you have my permission to rearrange your running shoes, preferably in an air-conditioned environment.

Hot weather slowdown for long runs

As the temperature rises above 55 °F (12 °C), your body starts to build up heat, but most runners aren't significantly slowed until 60 °F (14 °C). If you make the adjustments early, you won't have to suffer later and slow down a lot more at that time. The baseline for this table is 60°F or 14 °C.

- Between 60 °F and 64 °F:
  Slow down 30 seconds per mile slower than you would run at 60 °F.
- Between 14 °C and 16.5 °C:
  Slow down 20 seconds per kilometer than you would run at 14 °C.
- Between 65 °F and 69 °F:
  Slow down 1 minute per mile slower than you would run at 60 °F.
- Between 17 °C and 19.5 °C:
  Slow down 40 seconds per kilometer slower than you would run at 14 °C.
- Between 70 °F and 74 °F:
  Slow down 1:30 per mile slower than you would run at 60 °F.
- Between 20 °C and 22 °C:
  Slow down 1 minute per kilometer slower than you would run at 14 °C.
- Between 75 °F and 79 °F:
  Slow down 2 minutes per mile slower than you would run at 60 °F.
- Between 22.5 °C and 25 °C:
  Slow down 1:20 per kilometer slower than you would run at 14 °C.
- Above 80 °F and 25 °C:
  Be careful; take extra precautions to avoid heat disease.
- Or exercise indoors.
  Or arrange your shoes next to the air conditioner.

© Thinkstock/iStock

Heat disease alert!

While it is unlikely that you will push yourself into heat disease, the longer you are exercising in hot (or humid) conditions, the more you increase the likelihood of this dangerous medical situation. That's why I recommend breaking up your short maintenance runs into short segments when it's hot, if you must run outdoors for your short runs. Be sensitive to your reactions to the heat and those of the runners around you. When one of the symptoms is present, this is normally not a major problem unless there is significant distress. But when several are experienced, take action because heat disease can lead to death. I'm against death. It's always better to be conservative: Stop the workout and cool off.

Symptoms:

- Intense heat build-up in the head
- General overheating of the body
- Significant headache
- Significant nausea
- General confusion and loss of concentration
- Loss of muscle control
- Excessive sweating and then cessation of sweating
- Clammy skin
- Excessively rapid breathing
- Muscle cramps
- Feeling faint
- Unusual heart beat or rhythm
- Balance issues increase

Risk factors:

- Viral or bacterial infection
- Taking medication: especially cold medicines, diuretics, medicines for diarrhea, antihistamines, atropine, scopolamine, tranquilizers, even cholesterol and blood pressure medications. Check with your doctor on medication issues, especially when running in hot weather.
- Dehydration (especially due to alcohol)
- Severe sunburn
- Overweight
- Lack of heat training
- Exercising more than one is used to
- Occurrence of heat disease in the past
- Two or more nights of extreme sleep deprivation
- Certain medical conditions including high cholesterol, high blood pressure, extreme stress, asthma, diabetes, epilepsy, cardiovascular disease, smoking, or a general lack of fitness
- Drug use, including alcohol, over-the-counter medications, and prescription drugs (Consult with your doctor about using drugs when you are exercising hard in hot weather.)

Take action! Call 911

Use your best judgment, but in most cases anyone who exhibits two or more of the symptoms should get into a cool environment and get medical attention immediately. An extremely effective cool-off method is to soak towels, sheets, or clothing in cool or cold water and wrap them around the individual. If ice is available, sprinkle some ice over the wet cloth.

Chapter 28:
Your Motivation Training Plan

We are surrounded by a sea of stress. If we go with the flow of how we feel, we'll allow the subconscious brain to secrete anxiety and negative attitude hormones which will send our attitude rising and falling. Your mission is to have strategies in place to shift control into the executive brain in the frontal lobe for smooth and confident sailing.

By developing and using cognitive strategies, you can shift mental control away from the subconscious and into the executive brain. By following the methods in this chapter, you can train your brain to move from one thought to the next, just as you train your body to go one more mile or one more walk break. This manages the flow of negative hormones and turns on circuits to move you forward, step by step.

Throughout the day, most of the routine activities are monitored and managed by the subconscious, reflex brain. One of the key reflex functions is to monitor stress and start shutting things down (like motivation) when the stress level is too high. Having a plan in advance that you believe in will help you shift brain control into the frontal lobe—the conscious brain. Focusing on one small (and doable) step at a time reduces stress significantly as the frontal lobe keeps you focused on the next task. This brain component overrides the negativity of the reflex brain. By moving from one step to the next, you maintain conscious control over your motivation and your training, reprograming the subconscious brain to get moving, get out the door, keep going, break through barriers, and be strong to the finish. As you practice and fine-tune these cognitive strategies, the process becomes easier and easier.

Here are the major concepts:

- Do a reality check on your goal. Make sure that it is within your current capabilities and that you have enough time to perform the key workouts, while still resting between. Keep evaluating your goals and adjust as you head toward the key dates on your calendar. This maintains conscious control over the process.
- Acknowledge that the subconscious brain responds to stress by sending negative hormone messages to lower motivation. Under severe stress this reflex brain will reduce blood flow to gut, frontal lobe, and damaged areas to create pain. Start talking to the reflex brain when this starts to happen; laugh and tell it to open up the blood flow. This shifts brain activity into the executive brain where you can take conscious control.
- Diffuse the stress by using one or more of the simple methods listed next or one that you design. Keep telling the reflex brain that you know what it is doing and that you will not let this happen.
- Move forward by walking. Even if you are not going to run immediately, walk around the room thinking through the steps listed next. Use uplifting mantras that help you focus on the positive. This conscious mental shift can change your mood in a few minutes by triggering the release of positive peptides.
- When it is time for your run, go through the Jump Start program in the book *Mental Training for Runners: How to Stay Motivated*. As you Run-Walk-Run, the endorphins you release will lock into receiver sites all over the body, transmitting messages that you feel good and you can do it.
- During the run, or during other quiet periods (driving in a car, waiting for a flight, or a meeting) Identify the challenges you want to manage or overcome. List the negative messages you receive and the problems in past experiences. Then rehearse yourself through each situation.
- Concentrate on one challenge at a time. As you fine-tune your strategy, you will get better at moving quickly to positive action.
- Break up the challenge into a series of small steps that take you from the beginning of the challenge to the successful finish.

- Mentally rehearse the steps throughout the day. Even if you don't know the solution to problems that come up, rehearse yourself digging down, getting through it, and finishing with a great feeling of accomplishment.
- As you repeat and fine-tune the rehearsal, you are reprogramming the reflex brain to automatically move from one step to the next when confronted with the challenge.

As long as you have the challenge, continue the regular rehearsal, adjusting to your situation and becoming more and more effective.

Note: For more information on this topic with step-by-step instructions, see our book *Mental Training for Runners: How to Stay Motivated*, available autographed at www.JeffGalloway.com.

Chapter 29:
Mental Training Programs

You can gain control over your attitude, your performance and your pain.

- Training programs can reprogram the subconscious reflex brain.
- You have the power to take charge over motivation and improve attitude.
- Rehearsal drills break up a task into doable steps, performed step-by-step.
- Magic words tap into successful patterns and our intuitive, creative powers.
- Dirty tricks will distract your reflex brain; activate the frontal lobe.
- Then, you can manage and eliminate the way stress lowers your motivation.

The choice is yours: You can take control over your attitude, or you can let your reflex brain go through a series of negative reactions that usually result in low motivation and reduced performance. By using the proven strategies in this chapter, you can turn a negative attitude into a positive one, reprogram the reflex brain to stay on track to a positive goal, and tap into the incredible powers of the conscious right brain. Whether you struggle to get out the door when running by yourself, or you need more motivation to keep going down the trail when it's tough, you have a better chance of success when you have a strategy. This is your motivational training program.

To understand motivation, look inside the mental command and response center. When we are doing a habitual activity, like running, we tend to let the subconscious reflex brain keep things going. When stress accumulates to a significant level, this powerful center takes protective action to reduce motivation and lower effort level. It will trigger the release of negative attitude hormones which stimulate negative thoughts.

A stream of messages are released, telling us "slow down," "stop and you'll feel better," "this isn't your day," and even ask philosophical questions like "why are you doing this?" Stress secretions of peptides lock into sites all over the body, transmitting an emotional environment that is unmotivated and negative. Reflex brain also reduces blood flow to areas of damage that it has already identified. This results in a sensation of pain that normally would not be felt based upon the damage itself, a condition called Tension Myositis Syndrome (TMS).

Note: I am not suggesting that you should run through pain when there is chance of a serious injury. When you have pain in a weak link area that you suspect is an injury, check with your doctor to verify. In many cases, however, the pain is stress-induced TMS and can be managed.

By engaging the conscious brain in the frontal lobe, we can stay on track and possibly push to a higher level of performance—even when there is significant stress. The series of mental training drills in this chapter have been very successful in shifting control to the conscious brain and then reprogramming the reflex brain. With the conscious brain in charge, you can back off the effort if there is a legitimate issue of health or safety (very rare), or check your pace to ensure that your goal is not out of your current range of ability.

These mental training methods can allow you to move from one doable step to the next. By managing your pace and diffusing stress, the creative and intuitive right side of the frontal lobe can search for solutions to current problems, with connections to your inner resources, engaging the spirit.

Method #1

Rehearsing success

Individuals in various fields have used rehearsal for decades to achieve their potential on any given day. Mentally envisioning a series of challenges and rewards, all the way to the goal, gears up the mind–body team to work together at top capacity.

- Rehearsing realistic fatigue, aches and pains, negative messages, and doubts desensitizes you to the challenges.
- Break it into small steps. The conscious frontal lobe reprograms the reflex brain to stay focused by breaking down a challenge into segments, one leading automatically to the next to the successful finish.
- Rehearsal plans can reprogram the subconscious brain. As the rehearsal is repeated and fine-tuned, the reflex brain can be reprogrammed to move you from one positive step to the next, instead of responding to the negative motivation reflex due to stress and pressure.

Rehearsal drills are listed in the Situations chapter of my book *Mental Training for Runners: How to Stay Motivated*, with step-by-step formats.

What is the rehearsal drill: This is a mental storyline of how you want the experience to unfold. At first, you may focus on specific parts of a trail or workout or a race that has been challenging for you. You may continue to rehearse only the challenging parts or tie the parts into a continuous preview of the whole experience. Most runners fast forward through the less challenging segments and focus on the issues that have caused problems. Someone experienced with this drill can move through a marathon rehearsal within a matter of two to three minutes at the end of a season.

When: Rehearsals can be done during a run, when driving, in the shower, or waiting for a flight. Trying out the rehearsal during a hard workout can help you fine-tune it to be more effective. Many go through key rehearsal segments during long runs.

Be realistic and positive: The effectiveness of this mental drill will depend upon how complete and honest you were about the real challenges, how often and effective you rehearsed, and how open you are to making adjustments and digging deep as you get through the struggle. It's also important to visualize finishing with pride, satisfaction, and a great sense of accomplishment.

Desensitize: Revisit the negative messages that have been experienced during challenging workouts or races and every significant physical challenge that could happen during the event. As you rehearse getting through these, you desensitize yourself to surprises that could add stress during the event.

Rehearse the problem, even if you don't know the solution: By envisioning a past problem that you haven't solved, including digging down and getting through it, you empower the creative and intuitive right brain to find solutions. It often does this by race day (often without sending a message).

A series of small steps: Challenges are not confronted head-on, but segmented into doable units. When there is a significant hill that you are worried about, visualize shortening the run segments, shortening stride length, accomplishing one segment at a time, and not focusing on the top of the hill until you are congratulating yourself for moving over the top, smoothly gliding down the other side.

Each segment leads automatically to the next: By rehearsing the segments attached to one another, you are more likely to move from one to the next, when you get into the challenge.

Rehearse a variety of weather conditions and aches and pains: As you envision a variety of possible challenges, you will not only be better prepared for what could happen. You are training the various mind–body components to work as a team to get the job done, while making adjustments for the conditions of the day.

Finish with a vision of success and accomplishment: Always rehearse success that is realistic. Yes you feel tired, but you crossed the finish with strength and dignity. Focusing too specifically on a goal that is too ambitious can disconnect the brain circuits that could help you with doable performances.

Method #2

Magic words

Even the most motivated person has periods during a tough trail run or race when he or she wants to abandon the goal. By using a successful brainwashing technique, you can use the resources from past successes to pull you through these negative thoughts and feel like a champion at the end. Associate these successes with key words, and you can build on this success and confidence with each use.

Think back to the common and significant problems that you face in your tough workouts or races. These are the ones that are most likely to challenge you again. As you go through a series of tough trail treks and long runs, you will confront just about every problem you will face. Go back in your memory bank and pull out instances when you started to lose motivation due to these but finished and overcame the challenge.

My three magic words: Relax. Power. Glide.

In really tough runs, I have three challenges that occur over and over: 1) I become tense when I get really tired, worried that I will struggle badly at the end. 2) I feel the loss of the bounce and strength I had at the beginning and worry that there will be no strength later. 3) My form starts to get ragged and I worry about further deterioration of muscles and tendons and more fatigue due to wobbling.

The problems themselves are almost never serious. The key word is worry. When you focus on the negative possibilities, you stimulate negative hormones and build anxiety. This adds stress to the reflex brain, which will trigger more negative attitude peptides. So by focusing on problems and predicting negative outcomes, you will lose motivation and realize what you are projecting.

My big motivational breakthrough was learning to counter these three problems with the magic words: Relax. Power. Glide. The visualization of each of these positives shifts mental control to the conscious frontal lobe of the brain. The real magic comes from the association I have made with hundreds of successful experiences when I started to "lose it" in one of the three areas but overcame the problems. Each time I rehearse one or more of the challenges, I associate the experience with these magic words and add to the magic. Positive peptides are released, attitude improves, stress is overcome, and confidence returns.

Now, when something starts to go wrong, I repeat the three words over and over. Instead of increasing my anxiety, the repetition of the words calms me down (negative hormones are neutralized) and shifts me into my conscious brain. Even though I don't feel as strong in the last mile as I did in the first one, I've gained control just by knowing that I have a cognitive strategy and can draw upon my past experience (more positive-attitude hormones are secreted). And when my legs lose the efficient path and bounce, the right frontal lobe is empowered to take over and make adjustments and find inner strength to go on, as it has in past successes.

When I say magic words that are associated with successful experience, there are two positive effects. Saying the words floods the brain with positive memories. For a while, the negative messages of the left brain don't have a chance, and you can get down the trail for a half mile or more. The second effect may be more powerful. The words directly link you to the right brain, which works intuitively to make the same connections that allowed you solve the problems before.

To be successful on any day, you must first finish the race. Most of the time you can get through the bad parts by not giving up and simply putting one foot in front of the other. As you push beyond the negative left brain messages, you create the confidence to do this again and again. Each time you use the magic words and feel the results, you are maintaining conscious brain control and reprogramming the reflex brain. Feel free to use my magic words or develop your own. The more experiences you have associated with the words, the more magic.

Method #3

Playing dirty tricks on the reflex brain

The strategy of the rehearsal drill will get you focused and organized, while reducing the stress for at least the first third of the race or workout. Magic words can pull you along through most of the remaining challenging sessions. But on the really rough days, it helps to have some dirty tricks to play on the reflex brain.

These are quick fixes that distract the reflex brain's "garbage" messages for a while, allowing the conscious brain to take control. This allows you to keep going for the next segment of the course. These imaginative and sometimes crazy images don't have to have any logic behind them. But when you counter a reflex brain anxiety with a creative idea, you shift control into the frontal lobe, activating the creative right side. The flow of negative messages stops for a while.

The conscious action and the image of each trick, as mentioned next, will shift action to the executive brain where you can take command. This can change the peptides from negative to positive. Having fun with these visualizations will unlock more positive hormones, improving confidence and attitude.

A shift to creative images can increase activity in the right brain of your frontal lobe. This often triggers a series of creative thoughts that can entertain you. Once engaged, the right brain can subconsciously solve problems, boost your inner resolve to keep going, and find hidden strength.

Dirty trick: The giant invisible rubber band

When I get tired at the end of a hard race, I unpack this secret weapon and throw it around someone ahead of me or around someone who had the audacity to pass me. For a while, the person doesn't realize that he or she has been "looped" and continues to push onward while I get the mental benefit of being pulled along. After a minute or two of mentally projecting myself into this image, I have to laugh for believing in such an absurd notion. But when you take charge over the situation by projecting a set of behaviors and acting on them, you activate the conscious brain to take control. Furthermore, laughing switches on the creative, resourceful right side. This can generate several entertaining ideas, especially when you do this on a regular basis.

The right brain has millions of dirty and entertaining tricks. Once you get it rolling, you're likely to receive intuitive solutions to current problems. It can stimulate new thoughts as you get closer to your finish, step-by-step. Most important, this circuit can empower the legs, feet, and muscles to do what they are capable of doing on that day. The result will often surprise you.

More dirty tricks
- **The magnet on the mountain:**
  When you start to slow down while going up a hill, imagine that there is a huge magnet on the top that is pulling you up the hill.

- **Oxygen molecules in your shirt:**
  When you are feeling the fatigue from a hard run, tap your shirt three times and inhale. There are powerful oxygen molecules released that will help to revive your muscles.

- Bouncy air pads on your feet:
  During the last third of your race, when you feel that the feet aren't bouncing any more, turn on the mental switch that inserts air into the skin on the bottom of your feet. It is only activated if you shorten your stride and keep your feet low to the ground.

Note: In my book *Mental Training for Runners: How to Stay Motivated*, you'll find the mental coaching for the following situations:

- Getting out the door early in the morning
- Getting out the door after work, school, or a tough day
- Finishing a tough workout
- Doing the next segment
- Finishing a tough race
- Coming back from an injury
- Coming back from an illness
- Coming back from an extended layoff
- Coming back after a bad race or workout
- Burning more fat
- Coping when a close running friend moves away
- Reprogramming the reflex brain to use Run-Walk-Run

Chapter 30:
A Trail Runner's Diet

© Thinkstock/iStock

As an endurance athlete, you will not need a significant increase in vitamins and minerals or protein compared with a sedentary person. But if you don't get these ingredients for several days in a row, you will feel less energized and more tired. By following the provided guidelines and monitoring nutrition by an app or website, you can avoid running out of gas.

Most important resource: water

Whether you prefer water, juice, or other fluids, drink regularly throughout the day. Strive for 8 x 8 ounces (240 ml) during the day, more if you have returned from a long hot run. Caffeine drinks only deliver half of the fluid for absorption. Alcohol has a dehydrating effect.

If you have to take bathroom stops during walks or runs, you are drinking too much, either before or during the exercise. During an exercise session of 60 minutes or less, most exercisers don't need to drink at all. The intake of fluid before exercise should be arranged so that the excess fluid is eliminated before the run. Each person is a bit different, so you will have to find a routine that works for you. See the following guidelines.

Sweat the electrolytes

Electrolytes are the salts that your body loses when you sweat: sodium, potassium, magnesium, and calcium. When these minerals get too low, your fluid transfer system doesn't work as well and you may experience ineffective cooling, swelling of the hands, and other problems. Most runners have no problem replacing these in a normal diet, but if you are regularly experiencing cramping during or after exercise, and you are taking very liberal walk breaks from the beginning of your runs, you may be low in sodium or potassium. The best product I've found for replacing these minerals is called Succeed! If you have high blood pressure (or any issue with electrolytes), get your doctor's guidance before taking any salt supplement.

Practical eating issues

- Most of my runners have not needed to eat before a run, unless the blood sugar is low (see the next chapter).
- Before a long run or long race, drink a six-ounce glass of water as soon as you wake up. Don't drink until the run or the race begins.
- Reload most effectively by eating 100-300 calories within 30 minutes of finishing a run (80% carb/20% protein).
- During long runs and races, the rule of thumb is two to four ounces of water every two miles.
- Blood sugar booster rule of thumb during long runs and races: 30-40 calories every 2 miles. Use various snacks during long runs to find the one that works best for you: gummi bears, hard candy, gels, energy bars, or sugar cubes.
- Eating or drinking too much right before the start of a run can interfere with lower lung breathing, and may cause side pain. The food or fluid in your stomach limits your intake of air into the lower lungs and restricts the action of the diaphragm.
- If you are running low on blood sugar at the end of your long runs, increase your blood sugar booster snacks from the beginning of your next run (see the next chapter for more information).

- It is never a good idea to eat a huge meal, especially the night before a long run or a race. Those who claim that they must carb load with a large meal the night before are rationalizing their desire to eat a lot of food. Eating a big meal the night before (or the day of) a long run can result in "unloading" during the run.
- When you are sweating a lot, it is a good idea to drink one to two glasses a day of a good electrolyte beverage (not when running). Accelerade, by Pacific Health Labs is the best I've seen for both maintaining fluid levels and electrolyte levels.

Run-Walk eating schedule
- As soon as you wake, drink either a cup of coffee or a six-ounce glass of water.
- 30 minutes before any run (if blood sugar is low): consume approximately 100 calories of a blood sugar booster snack.
- Within 30 minutes after a run: consume approximately 100 to 300 calories of an 80% carb/20% protein snack (e.g., Endurox R4).
- If you are sweating a lot during hot weather, drink two to three glasses of a good electrolyte beverage like Accelerade throughout the day plus your normal intake of water (6-8 glasses is recommended).

Hint: Caffeine, when consumed before exercise, engages the systems that enhance running and extend endurance, but only half of the fluid will be absorbed.

Chapter 31:
Good Blood Sugar Level = Happy Trails

Your brain is fueled by blood sugar. When the blood sugar level (BSL) is at a good, moderate, normal level, you feel stable and motivated. But if the BSL is lowered or interrupted, the brain starts shutting things down, stimulating negative attitude hormones.

© Thinkstock/iStock

When blood sugar level is maintained throughout the day, you will be more motivated to exercise, add other movement to your life, be mentally active, deal with stress, and solve problems. Just as eating throughout the day keeps metabolism up, the steady infusion of balanced nutrients all day long will maintain stable BSL. This produces a feeling of well-being.

Before a run: You want to have a BSL that is in the normal range. If it is a bit too low you might feel hungry, lethargic, or tired. When you run in this condition, the increased need for energy can result in even lower blood sugar and a miserable run. But if you eat too much sugar, 45 or more minutes before you run, your BSL can rise too high. You'll feel really good for a short period, but the excess sugar triggers a release of insulin. This reduces BSL to an uncomfortable level. In this state your energy drops, mental focus is foggy, and motivation goes down rapidly.

For best results in raising blood sugar when it is too low (within 30 minutes before a run), a snack should have about 80% of the calories in simple carbohydrate and 20% in protein. This promotes the production of a manageable level of insulin, which is helpful before a run in getting the glycogen into your muscles and ready for use. The product Accelerade has worked best among the thousands of runners I hear from every year. It has the 80%/20% ratio of carb to protein. If you eat an energy bar with the 80/20 ratio, be sure to drink four to six ounces of water with it.

During trail runs: By testing various BSL snacks and planning ahead, you can be prepared for each trail trek. On short runs of about 90 minutes or less, most of my runners have not found it necessary to eat. There are individual issues, but BSL-boosting snacks are generally beneficial on runs of two hours or more. You don't want to get on the bad side of your BSL. Low levels are a stress on the brain, literally messing with your mind. If you have not eaten for several hours before a trail run, you'll receive an increase in the number of negative and anxiety hormones, reducing motivation to exercise or to finish the run.

The BSL roller coaster

Eating a snack with too many calories of simple carbohydrate can be counter-productive for BSL maintenance. As previously mentioned, when the sugar level gets too high, your body produces insulin, sending BSL lower than before. The tendency is to eat again, which produces excess calories that are converted into fat. But if you don't eat, you'll stay hungry and pretty miserable—in no mood to exercise or move around and burn calories or get in your run for the day.

Try eating every two to three hours

Once it is established which snacks work best to maintain your BSL, most people maintain a stable blood sugar level by eating small meals regularly every two to three hours. It's best to combine complex carbs with about 20 to 25% of the calories in protein and a small amount of fat (10-20% of the calories of that snack).

Do I have to eat before running?

Only if your blood sugar is low. Most who run in the morning don't need to eat anything before the start. As already mentioned, if your blood sugar level is low in the afternoon and you have a run scheduled, a snack can help when taken about 30 minutes or less before the run. If you feel that a morning snack will help, the only issue is to avoid consuming so much that you get an upset stomach.

Eating during exercise

Most exercisers don't need to worry about eating or drinking during a run until the length exceeds 90 minutes. At this point, there are several options. In this case, my rule of thumb is to take 30 to 40 calories every two miles. Diabetics may need to eat sooner and more often, but this is an individual issue.

The brain's fuel is blood glucose. If you don't keep this boosted during a long run, the brain will be deprived and will start shutting things down. Avoid this by trying different snacks and amounts, using the formula that works best for you.

Rule of thumb: 30 to 40 calories about every two miles (20-25 minutes), with 2 to 4 ounces of water (60-120 ml).

GU or Gel products: These come in small packets and are the consistency of honey or thick syrup. The most successful way to take them is to put one to three packets in a small plastic bottle with a pop-top. About every 10-15 minutes, take a small amount with a sip or two of water. The Fitlethic ifitness belt has easy-to-use bottles.

Energy bars: Cut into small pieces. Avoid products with a lot of fiber, fat, or protein.

Candy: Particularly gummy bears or hard candies, such as LifeSavers.

Sugar cubes, LifeSavers, gummy bears: This is the simplest of the BSL booster snacks and the easiest on the stomach for most runners.

Sports drinks: I've noticed that a significant percentage of my runners experience nausea when they drink sports drinks during a run, so I recommend water. During heavy periods of training it's a good idea to have a pitcher of a good electrolyte beverage like Accelerade in the fridge, so you can drink 8 to 16 ounces a day, especially during hot weather. If you are going to be running for more than seven hours, it could be helpful to have two to four ounces of an electrolyte beverage every 30 minutes or so—or use a buffered salt tablet like S!Caps. Try several on different training runs to see which settles best in your digestive tract.

It is important to reload after exercise within 30 minutes.

Whenever you have finished a hard or long workout (for you), a recovery snack can help you recover faster. Again, the 80%/20% ratio of simple carbohydrate to protein has been most successful in reloading the muscles. The product that has worked best among the thousands I work with each year is Endurox R4.

Chapter 32:
Troubleshooting

© Thinkstock/jStock

- **Coming back after a layoff from running**
- **It hurts!**
- **No energy...**
- **Side pain**
- **I feel great one day; but the next day...**
- **No motivation**
- **Cramps in my leg muscles**
- **Upset stomach or diarrhea**
- **Headache**
- **Should I run when I have a cold?**

How do I start back when I've had time off?

The longer you've been away from running, the slower you must plan for your return. I want to warn you now that you will reach a point when you feel totally back in shape, but you are not. There are many terrain adaptations that you must bring back gradually. Stay with the following plan for your return and when in doubt, be more conservative. Remember that you are in this for the long run!

Less than two weeks off: You will feel like you are starting over again but should come back quickly. Let's say that you were at week #10 but had to take 10 days off. Start back at week #2 for the first week. If all is well, skip to #3 or #4 for the second week. If that works well, gradually transition over the next two to three weeks back to the schedule you were using before you had your layoff.

14 days to 29 days off: You will also feel like you are starting over again, and it will take longer to get it all back. Within about five to six weeks you should be back to normal. Use the schedule of your choice (from week #1) for two weeks. If there are no aches, pains, or lingering fatigue, then use the schedule but skip every other week. After the 5th week, transition back into what you were doing before the break.

One month or more off: If you have not run for a month or more, start over again like a beginner. Use one of the schedules in this book, following it exactly (from week #1) for the first few weeks. After two to three weeks, the safest plan is to continue with the schedule. If you're having no aches and pains and no lingering fatigue, you could increase more rapidly by skipping one week out of three. After two months of no problems, your conditioning can often be back to pre-injury levels.

Remember that you can walk most or all of the long runs. You will receive the same endurance from a long walk as from a long run. So when you miss a long run, you can catch up by walking most or all of the next long run. If you are going to be running some of that run, the best strategy is to walk the first portion. If you are very tired at the end, try to walk gently and slowly and finish the distance.

It hurts! Is it just a passing ache, or a real injury?

Most of the aches and pains felt when running will go away within a minute or two. If the pain comes on during a run, just walk for an additional two minutes, jog a few strides, and walk another two minutes. If the pain comes back after doing this four or five times, stop running and walk. If the pain does not go away when you walk, stop!

Walking pain: When the pain stays around when walking, try a very short stride. Walk for 30 to 60 seconds. If it still hurts when walking, try sitting down and massaging the area that hurts, if you can. Sit for two to four minutes.

When you try again to walk, and it still hurts, call it a day. Your workout is over.

It's an injury if...

There's inflammation or swelling in the area.

There's loss of function; the foot or knee doesn't work correctly.

There's pain. It hurts and keeps hurting or even gets worse.

Treatment suggestions:

- See a doctor who has treated other runners very successfully and wants to get you back on the road or trail.
- Take at least two to five days off from any activity that could irritate the area to get the healing started—more if needed.
- If the injury site is close to the skin (tendon, foot), rub a chunk of ice on the area(s), constantly rubbing for 15 minutes until the area gets numb. Continue to do this for a week after you feel no symptoms. Ice bags and gel ice do no good at all in most cases.
- If the problem is inside a joint or muscle, call your doctor and ask if you can use prescription strength anti-inflammatory medication. Don't take any medication without a doctor's advice—and follow that advice.
- If you have a muscle injury, see a veteran sports massage therapist. Try to find one who has a lot of successful experience treating the area where you are injured. A massage therapist's magic fingers and hands can often work wonders.
- Sometimes the injury will heal enough to allow running on pavement but not on trails. Uneven terrain can aggravate an injury, so stay on solid ground until the injury can handle it.

This is advice from one runner to another. For more info on injuries and treatment, see a doctor and read *Running Injuries: Treatment and Prevention* by Dr. David Hannaford and me.

I have no energy today.

There will be a number of days each year when you will not feel like exercising. On most of these, you can turn it around and feel great. Occasionally, you will not be able to do this, because of an infection, lingering fatigue, or other physical problems. Here's a list of things that can give you energy. If these actions don't lead you to a run, then read the nutrition sections—particularly the blood sugar chapter in this book, or our book *Running & Fat Burning for Women.*

- Eat an energy bar, with water or caffeinated beverage, about 30 minutes before the run. Caffeine helps!
- Or, half an hour before exercising you could drink approximately 100 calories of a sports drink that has a mix of 80% simple carbohydrate and 20% protein. The product Accelerade already has this ratio.
- Just walk for five minutes away from your house or office, and the energy often kicks in. Forward movement gets the attitude moving, too. Once one starts walking down a trail, the motivation often picks up.
- One of the prime reasons for no energy is that you didn't reload within 30 minutes after your last exercise session: consume 200 to 300 calories of a mix that is 80% simple carbohydrate and 20% protein (Endurox R4 is the product that has this formulation).
- Low-carb diets will result in low energy to get motivated before a workout and often no energy to finish the workout. Blood sugar boosting (as noted in the previous chapter) may help.
- In most cases it is fine to keep going even if you aren't energetic. But if you sense an infection, see a doctor. If the low energy stays around for several days, see a nutritionist that knows about the special needs of exercisers or get some blood work done. This may be due to inadequate iron, B vitamins, or energy stores.

Note: If you have any problems with caffeine, don't consume any products containing it. As always, if you sense any health problem, see a doctor.

I have side pain.

This is very common and usually has a simple fix. Normally it is not anything to worry about, it just hurts. This condition is due to 1) the lack of lower lung breathing and 2) going a little too fast from the beginning of the run. You can correct #2 easily by walking more at the beginning and slowing down your running pace.

Lower lung breathing from the beginning of a run has prevented side pain in a high percentage of cases I've seen. This way of inhaling air is performed by diverting the air you breathe into your lower lungs. Also called belly breathing, this is how we breathe when asleep, and it provides maximum opportunity for oxygen absorption. If you don't do this from the beginning of a run, you are not getting the oxygen you need, the side pain will tell you. By slowing down, walking, and breathing deeply for a while, the pain may go away. But sometimes it does not. Most runners just continue to run and walk with the side pain. In over 50 years of running and helping others run, I've not seen any lasting negative effect from those who run with a side pain.

You don't have to take in a maximum breath to perform this technique. Simply breathe a normal breath but send it to the lower lungs. You know that you have done this if your stomach goes up and down as you inhale and exhale. If your chest goes up and down, you are breathing shallowly.

Note: Never breathe in and out rapidly. This can lead to hyperventilation, dizziness, and fainting.

I feel great one day...and not the next

If you can solve this problem, you could become a very wealthy person. There are a few common reasons for this, but there will always be "those days" when the body doesn't seem to work right—the gravity seems heavier than normal—and you cannot find a reason.

- Pushing through. In most cases, this is a one-day occurrence. Most runners just put more walking into the mix and get through it. Before pushing, however, make sure that you don't have a medical reason why you feel bad. Don't exercise when you have a lung infection, for example.
- Heat and humidity will make you feel worse. You will often feel great when the temperature is below 60 °F and miserable when it is 80 °F or above (especially at the end of the workout).
- Low blood sugar can make any run a bad run. You may feel good at the start and suddenly feel like you have no energy. Every step seems to take a major effort. Read about this topic in chapter 31.
- Low motivation. Use the rehearsal techniques in chapter 28 to get you out the door on a bad day. These have helped numerous runners turn their minds around—even in the middle of a run.
- Infection can leave you feeling lethargic, achy, and unable to run at the same pace that was easy a few days earlier. Check the normal signs (fever, chills, swollen lymph glands) and at least call your doctor if you suspect something.
- Medication and alcohol, even when taken the day before, can leave a hangover that dampens a workout.
- A slower start can make the difference between a good day and a bad day. When your body is on the edge of fatigue or other stress, it only takes a few seconds too fast per mile, walking or running, to push into discomfort or worse.

My muscles cramp

At some point, most trail runners will experience cramps. These muscle contractions usually occur in the feet or the calf muscles and may come during a run or walk, or they may hit at random. Most commonly, they will occur at night or when you are sitting around at your desk or watching TV in the afternoon or evening.

Cramps vary in severity. Most are mild but some can shut down the muscles and hurt when they seize up. Massage and a short, gentle movement of the muscle can help to bring most of the cramps around. Odds are that stretching will make the cramp worse or tear the muscle fibers.

Most cramps are due to overuse, exercising farther or faster than in the recent past, or continuing to put yourself at your limit, especially in warm weather. Look at the pace and distance of your runs and walks in your training journal to see if you have been running too far, too fast, or both.

- Continuous running increases cramping. Taking walk breaks more often can reduce or eliminate cramps. Many runners who used to cramp when they ran a minute and walked a minute stopped cramping with a ratio of run 20-30 seconds and walk 30-60 seconds.
- During hot weather, a good electrolyte beverage can help to replace the salts that your body loses in sweating. A drink like Accelerade, for example, can help to top off these minerals when you drink approximately six to eight ounces every one to two hours during your workday.
- On very long hikes, walks, or runs, however, the continuous sweating, especially when drinking a lot of fluid, can push your sodium levels too low and produce muscle cramping. If you are mostly walking and are still experiencing cramps, a buffered salt tablet, like Succeed!, has helped greatly.
- Many medications, especially those designed to lower cholesterol, have muscle cramps as one of their known side effects. Runners who use medications and cramp should ask their doctor if there are alternatives.

Here are several ways of dealing with cramps:

- Take a longer and more gentle warm-up.
- Shorten your run segment.
- Shorten your stride, whether running or walking.
- Slow down your walk, and walk more.
- Shorten your distance on a hot or humid day.
- Break your run up into two segments.
- Look at any other exercise that could be causing the cramps.
- Take a buffered salt tablet at the beginning of your exercise.
- Shorten your stride—especially on hills.
- **Note:** If you have high blood pressure, ask your doctor before taking any salt product.

© Thinkstock/iStock

I have upset stomach or diarrhea

Sooner or later, virtually every runner has at least one episode with nausea or diarrhea (N/D). It comes from the build-up of total stress that you accumulate. Most commonly, it is the stress of running on that day due to the causes listed below. But stress can come from many unique conditions within the individual. Your body triggers the N/D to get you to reduce the exercise, which will reduce the stress.

Here are the common causes:

- Running too fast or too far is the most common cause. Runners are confused about this, because the pace doesn't feel too fast in the beginning. Each person has a level of fatigue that triggers these conditions. Slowing down and taking more walk breaks will help you manage the problem.
- Eating too much or too soon before the run. Your system has to work hard when you're running, and it works hard to digest food. Doing both at the same time raises stress and results in nausea. Having food in your stomach in the process of being digested is an extra stress and a likely target for elimination.
- Eating a high-fat, high-fiber, or high-protein diet. Even one meal that has over 50% of the calories in fat or protein can lead to N/D hours later.
- Eating too much the afternoon or evening on the day before. A big evening meal will still be in the gut the next morning, being digested. When you bounce up and down on a run, which you will, you add stress to the system, often producing (N/D).
- Heat and humidity are a major cause of these problems. Some people don't adapt to heat well and experience N/D with minimal build-up of temperature or humidity. But in hot conditions, everyone has a core body temperature increase that will result in significant stress to the system, often causing nausea and sometimes diarrhea. By slowing down, taking more walk breaks, and pouring water over your head, you can manage this. The best time to exercise in warm weather is before the sun rises above the horizon.

- Drinking too much water before or during a run. If you have too much water in your stomach, and you are bouncing around, you put stress on the digestive system. Reduce your intake to the bare minimum. Most runners don't need to drink any fluid before a run that is 60 minutes or less.
- Drinking too much of a sugar or electrolyte drink. Water is the easiest substance for the body to process. The addition of sugar or electrolyte minerals, as in a sports drink, makes the substance harder to digest for many runners. During a run (especially on a hot day), it is best to drink only water. Cold water is best.
- Drinking too much fluid too soon after a run. Even if you are very thirsty, don't gulp down large quantities of any fluid. Try to drink no more than six to eight ounces every 20 minutes or so. If you are particularly prone to N/D, just take two to four sips every five minutes or so. When the body is very stressed and tired, it's not a good idea to consume a sugar drink. The extra stress of digesting the sugar can lead to problems.
- Don't let running be stressful to you. Some runners get too obsessed about getting their run in or running at a specific pace. This adds stress to your life. Relax and let your run diffuse some of the other tensions in your life.

I get headaches when I run

There are several reasons why runners get headaches on runs. While uncommon, they happen to the average runner about one to five times a year. The extra stress running puts on the body can trigger a headache on a tough day—even considering the relaxation that comes from the run. Many runners find that a dose of an over-the-counter headache medication takes care of the problem. As always, consult with your doctor about use of medication.

Here are the causes and their solutions:

- **Dehydration:** If you run in the morning, make sure that you hydrate well the day before—and rehydrate gradually afterward. Avoid alcohol if you run in the mornings and have headaches. Also watch the salt in your dinner meal the night before. A good sports drink like Accelerade, taken throughout the day the day before, will help to keep your fluid levels and your electrolytes topped off. If you run in the afternoon, follow the same advice leading up to your run on the day of the run.
- **Medication:** Medications can often produce dehydration. There are some medications that make runners more prone to headaches. Check with your doctor.
- **Too hot for you:** Run at a cooler time of the day (usually in the morning, before the sun rises above the horizon). When on a hot run, pour water over your head.
- **Pollen, asthma, allergies:** At certain times of the year, those who have allergies tend to get headaches. Check with your doctor about inhalers and allergy medicine.
- **Running a little too fast:** Start all runs more slowly, and walk more during the first half of the run.
- **Running farther than you have run in the recent past:** Monitor your mileage and don't increase more than about 15% farther than you have run on any single run in the past week.
- **Low blood sugar level:** Be sure that you boost your BLS with a snack about 30 to 60 minutes before you run. If you are used to having it, caffeine in a beverage can sometimes help this situation.

- **If prone to migraines:** Generally avoid caffeine, and try your best to avoid dehydration. Talk to your doctor about other possibilities.
- **Watch your neck and lower back:** If you have a slight forward lean as you run, you can put pressure on the spine, particularly in the neck and lower back. Read chapter 14 on running form and run upright.

Should I run when I have a cold?

There are so many individual health issues with a cold that you must talk with a doctor before you exercise when you have an infection. Usually you will be given the okay to gently exercise.

Lung infection: Don't run! A virus in the lungs can move into the heart and kill you. Lung infections are usually indicated by coughing.

Common cold: There are many infections that initially seem to be a normal cold but are not. At least call your doctor's office to get clearance before running. Be sure to explain how much you are running and what, if any, medication you are taking.

Throat infection and above: Most runners will be given the okay, but check with the doctor.

© Thinkstock/iStock

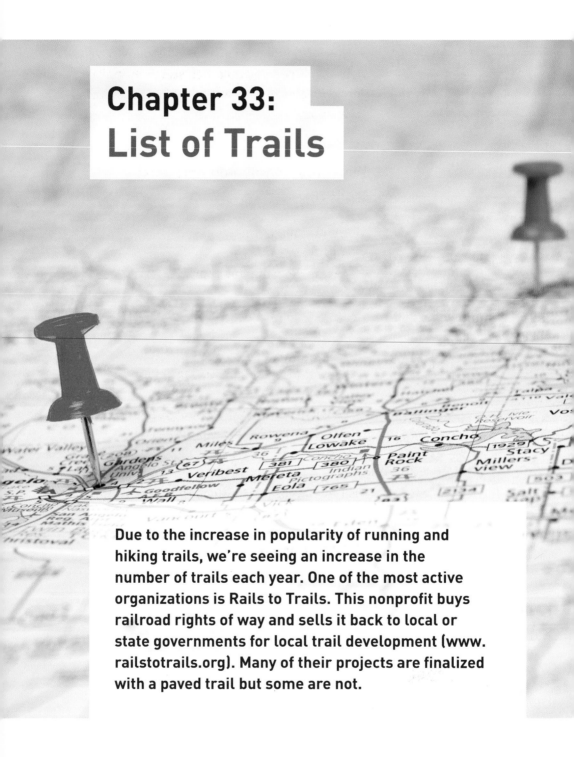

Chapter 33: List of Trails

Due to the increase in popularity of running and hiking trails, we're seeing an increase in the number of trails each year. One of the most active organizations is Rails to Trails. This nonprofit buys railroad rights of way and sells it back to local or state governments for local trail development (www. railstotrails.org). Many of their projects are finalized with a paved trail but some are not.

© Thinkstock/Hemera

A growing number of park departments have websites. When you do a web search for trails, you will often find a website with maps and access points.

Websites to help you find local trails:

- www.traillink.com
- trails.gorp.com
- www.seriousrunning.com
- www.trails.com
- www.alltrails.com
- www.trailrunners.org
- www.americantrails.org
- www.tripleblaze.com/Hiking-Trails
- www.trailsource.com
- en.wikiloc.com/trails/running/united-states—Individuals can post trails with description.

Visit the websites for the Appalachian Trail and the Pacific Crest Trail. Both are over 1,000 miles long and have many access points. Some segments will bring you into remote areas.

Trails that have been recommended by other runners:

Alabama
- www.alapark.com/Trails
- www.traillink.com/stateactivity/al-running-trails.aspx
- www.trails.com/toptrails.aspx?area = 10048
- Pelham—Oak Mountain State Park
- www.alapark.com/oakmountain/

Alaska
- www.alaska.org
- www.alaska.com/hiking
- www.trails.com/stateactivity.aspx?area = 10049
- www.seriousrunning.com/Trail-Running/Alaska_12.html
- www.traillink.com/stateactivity/ak-running-trails.aspx
- www.anchorage.net/ak/trails
- www.ketchikanalaska.com/adventure/hikingtrails.html

Arizona
- www.trails.com/findarea.aspx?state = AZ
- www.traillink.com/trailsearch.aspx?state = AZ
- www.seriousrunning.com/Trail-Running/Arizona_13.html
- www.aztrail.org
- www.arizonahikingtrails.com
- Grand Canyon—South Rim Trail
- Phoenix—There are a number of desert preserves with trails in the metro area. Do a web search for the parks in your area.
- Sedona—Red Rocks: a variety but try Bell Rock trail: www.sedonahikingtrails.com/bell-rock_trail.htm
- Phoenix area (Fountain Hills)—Pemberton Trail in the McDowell Mountain Regional Park: Recommend clockwise for an uphill first half, then downhill. Mostly smooth with relatively small rocky segments.

Arkansas

- www.traillink.com/stateactivity/ar-hiking-trails.aspx
- www.seriousrunning.com/Trail-Running/Arkansas_14.html
- www.trails.com/stateactivity.aspx?area = 10007
- www.arkansasstateparks.com/things-to-do/trails
- Allison—Sylamore Trail: A 23-mile point-to-point in the Ozarks. www.ouachitamaps. com/Sylamore%20Trail.html
- Bentonville—www.bentonvillear.com/parks_trails_pathways.html

California

- www.traillink.com/state/ca-trails.aspx
- www.trails.com/stateactivity.aspx?area = 13049
- www.trails.com/stateactivity.aspx?area = 14607
- www.seriousrunning.com/Trail-Running/California_15.html
- trailrunners.org/
- Santa Monica—Fire trails in the Santa Monica mountains. Sycamore Cove fire road is recommended by Steve Alnwick.
- Tahoe City—Dollar Hill Nordic Trails, north of Tahoe City.
- Auburn—Auburn State Recreational Area
- Lake Tahoe—www.tahoerimtrail.org
- Lompoc Mission—Beautiful trails
- Marin County—North Bolinas Coastal Trail into Point Reyes National Park
- Marin County—Tennessee Valley Trail
- Marin County—Mount Tamalpais trail system
- Orange County—www.ocparks.com: Westin Galloway recommends the Aliso and Wood Canyons Park, Crystal Cove State Park (including Laguna Beach), and Peters Canyon.
- Point Reyes National Park—Trails throughout this beautiful seacoast area
- North of Bodega Bay (on the coast west of Santa Rosa)—Shell Beach to Goat Rock
- Oakland—Redwood Regional Park: Especially the Canyon Meadows Trail through the redwoods.www.ebparks.org/parks/redwood
- Sacramento—A great system of trails (paved, gravel, and dirt) along the two rivers
- Woodside (west side, San Francisco Bay area)—Huddart Park: Scenic and tree covered

- Walnut Creek (east side, San Francisco Bay area)—MT Diablo: Good views, with many miles of fire roads and trails.
- San Diego area—Los Penesquitos Canyon: Great variety, gorgeous and peaceful.

Colorado
- www.coloradotrail.org—Hope Pass trail is recommended
- www.trails.com/stateactivity.aspx?area = 10017
- www.trails.com/findarea.aspx?state = CO
- www.traillink.com/trailsearch.aspx?state = CO
- Aspen—Triangle Pass trail
- Boulder—Mesa trail: 6 miles one way. Also check out Chautauqua Park Trailhead, and look at the other trails listed at www.protrails.com.
- Colorado Springs—Barr Trail up Pike's Peak: en.wikipedia.org/wiki/Barr_Trail; farrunner.com/
- Near Colorado Springs—Red Rocks, Garden of the Gods;Williams Canyon and Waldo Canyon. See www.cospringstrails.com\hikes\williams.
- Ouray—Perimeter Trail

Connecticut
- www.ct.gov/dot/cwp/view.asp?a = 3535&q = 259678—Trail list with maps
- www.cttrailrunning.com—CT trail database with other links
- www.trails.com/findarea.aspx?state = CT
- www.traillink.com/stateactivity/ct-hiking-trails.aspx
- www.tripleblaze.com/Hiking-Trails/Connecticut_10.html
- East Hampton—Airline Trail: Just off CT Route 2 on the south side of the road. This is a great running rail trail—solid surface, no pavement.

Delaware
- www.destateparks.com/activities/trails/hiking/index.asp
- www.trails.com/stateactivity.aspx?area = 10051
- www.trailsource.com/scripts/three.asp?STATENAME = DELAWARE&TYPE = HIKE
- www.tripleblaze.com/best/?c = 11

District of Columbia

- www.trails.gorp.com/TrailSearch?state = DC
- www.trails.com/stateactivity.aspx?area = 12845
- www.traillink.com/stateactivity/dc-running-trails.aspx
- Georgetown—C & O Canal Towpath
- Potomac River trails on west side of the river from downtown to Mt Vernon
- www.bikewashington.org

Florida

- www.dep.state.fl.us/gwt/default.htm—Various trails with maps
- floridatrailrunning.com/trails.html—Various trails with maps
- www.floridatrail.org
- www.traillink.com/stateactivity/fl-running-trails.aspx
- www.trails.com/toptrails.aspx?state = FL
- Blue Mountain Beach—Galloway retreats use this train system of hundreds of miles between Destin and Panama City.
- Fort Clinch Trail—www.floridastateparks.org/fortclinch/activities.cfm#22
- Gainesville—San Felasco Hammock Nature Preserve State Park
- Oscar Scherer State Park
- Stuart—Halpatiokee trail
- Lakeland—Circle B Bar Reserve: A nature preserve of Polk County.

Georgia

- Kennesaw Mountain, Chickamauga
- www.traillink.com/stateactivity/ga-running-trails.aspx
- www.seriousrunning.com/Trail-Running/Georgia_21.html
- www.georgiatrails.com
- www.run100miles.com/georgia-trail-running
- www.atlantatrails.com
- Chickamauga National Battlefield Park—A battlefield during the Civil War; this has a number of recreational trails and roads with little traffic and is located south of the Tennessee state line in northwest Georgia.
- Marietta—Kennesaw Mountain Battlefield Park: Great running on about 16 miles of trails.

- Sandy Springs/East Marietta—Columns Drive/Cochran Shoals: North of Atlanta along Chattahoochee River (National Park). There's an approximately 3-mile loop on the flat and several miles of forest trails with some hills.
- Savannah—Skidaway Island: Scenic and flat with variety.
- Douglasville—Sweetwater Creek State Park: Scenic with various degrees of difficulty.

Hawaii
- www.dcnr.state.pa.us/stateparks/recreation/hiking/index.htmHawaii
- hawaiistateparks.org/hiking/
- www.trails.com/stateactivity.aspx?area = 10015
- thebackpacker.com/trails/hi/
- www.tripleblaze.com/Hiking-Trails/Hawaii_15.html

Idaho
- www.trails.idaho.gov
- www.trails.com/findarea.aspx?state = ID
- www.traillink.com/stateactivity/id-hiking-trails.aspx
- Boise—stevestuebner.com/books/boise-trail-guide.htm: A good resource but must pay for maps.
- North Idaho Centennial Trail—Beautiful trail along Lake Coeur d'Alene and the Spokane River: www.northidahocentennialtrail.org

Indiana
- www.indianatrails.com
- www.southernindianatrails.freehostia.com
- www.in.gov/dnr/outdoor/4240.htm
- www.trails.com/toptrails.aspx?state = IN
- www.traillink.com/stateactivity/in-hiking-trails.aspx
- Avon—Avon-Washington Township Park (west of Indianapolis): Limited number of trails.
- Plainfield—Sodalis Nature Park: 3.5 miles of nature trails near hotels.
- Indianapolis—Eagle Creek Park: 22 miles of meandering trails.
- Nashville—Yellowwood State Forest: Lots of options, from Visitor Center.
- Martinsville—Morgan-Monroe State Forest: Many options.

Iowa

- www.icgov.org/default/?id = 1055
- www.iowatrails.net/resources
- www.trails.com/toptrails.aspx?state = IA
- www.tripleblaze.com/Hiking-Trails/Iowa_19.html
- www.seriousrunning.com/Trail-Running/Iowa_26.html

Illinois

- fpdcc.com/preserves-and-trails/maps/—Forest preserve areas of Cook County.
- www.traillink.com/stateactivity/il-running-trails.aspx
- alltrails.com/us/illinois/trail-running
- www.trails.com/toptrails.aspx?state = IL
- www.citra.ivs.org—Mostly trail races but offers contacts
- www.reconnectwithnature.org/recreation/Hiking-Running—Forest preserve of Will County
- dnr.state.il.us/lands/landmgt/parks
- Warrenville—Blackwell Forest Preserve: 9 miles of scenic trails with connection to the Prairie Trail. Avoid the hilltop loop.

Kansas

- www.traillink.com/stateactivity/ks-running-trails.aspx
- www.trails.com/findarea.aspx?state = KS
- www.trailsofkansas.com/kansashikingtrails.html
- www.thebackpacker.com/trails/ks/

Kentucky

- www.trails.com/toptrails.aspx?state = KY
- www.traillink.com/stateactivity/ky-running-trails.aspx
- www.thebackpacker.com/trails/ky/
- Land Between the Lakes, KY—Several trails including the Honker Trail.
- Lexington, KY—www.lexingtonky.gov/index.aspx?page = 262
- www.shakervillageky.org/The_Nature_Preserve/Hiking_Biking

Louisiana

- www.crt.state.la.us/parks/TrailsChart.htm
- www.louisianatrails.org/traillocation.html
- www.trails.com/findarea.aspx?state = LA
- www.traillink.com/stateactivity/la-hiking-trails.aspx

Maine

- www.mainetrailfinder.com
- www.maineoutdoors.com/hiking/hike_info_trails.shtml
- www.trails.com/findarea.aspx?state = ME
- www.traillink.com/stateactivity/me-hiking-trails.aspx
- www.seriousrunning.com/Trail-Running/Maine_30.html
- Acadia National Park, Bar Harbor.
- New Gloucester—Henning Pineland Farms: 15 miles of trails.

Maryland

- www.dnr.state.md.us/land/MD_Trails/Trails_in_MD.asp
- www.trails.com/toptrails.aspx?state = MD
- www.mdmountainside.com/attraction/great_allegheny_passage
- www.traillink.com/stateactivity/md-running-trails.aspx
- Cumberland—Great Alleghany Trail
- Tow Path—From Washington, D.C., Georgetown.

Massachusetts

- www.mass.gov/portal/tourism/outdoor/hiking/
- www.mass.gov/dcr/recreate/trails.htm
- www.traillink.com/stateactivity/ma-running-trails.aspx
- www.trails.com/toptrails.aspx?state = MA
- Boston—Asphalt trail along the Charles River in downtown area.
- Mount Greylock

Michigan

- trailsmichigan.com/index.html
- www.michigan.gov/dnr/0,1607,7-153-10365_16839---,00.html

- www.michigantrails.org/map
- www.traillink.com/state/mi-trails.aspx
- www.trails.com/toptrails.aspx?state = MI
- Grand Island in upper Michigan—Varied terrain.
- Marquette,—marquette.ifindtrail.com/
- Paradise—Taqua trail: Variety of terrain and footing.
- Shelby Township—Stoney Creek Trail: Several options including a 6-mile loop around a beautiful lake on a paved path.
- Rochester—Lake Orion; Paint Creek Trail: 10 miles point-to-point.
- Upper Peninsula—Escarpment trail in the Porcupine Mountain State Park. www.michigandnr.com/parksandtrails

Minnesota

- www.trails.com/findarea.aspx?state = MN
- www.traillink.com/state/mn-trails.aspx
- www.seriousrunning.com/Trail-Running/Minnesota_34.html
- www.dnr.state.mn.us/state_trails/index.html
- www.exploreminnesota.com/things-to-do/outdoors-nature/hiking/index.aspx
- Duluth—www.duluthmn.gov/parks/trail_listing.cfm
- Minneapolis—Numerous paved trails around lakes and throughout the metro area. Lake of the Isles is a favorite and is near the downtown area. www.mineapolisparks.org
- www.bloomingtonmn.org/page/1/activity-detail.jsp?id = 2228&name = Chain%20 of%20Lakes&type = Outdoor%20Activities#.UXKhGcrWkuM
- Lake Superior Trail—From Duluth to the Canadian border: www.shta.org
- Rochester—www.rochestermn.gov/departments/park/trails/index.asp
- Mankato—www.mankato-mn.gov/Trails/Page.aspx

Mississippi

- www.traillink.com/stateactivity/ms-running-trails.aspx
- www.trails.com/toptrails.aspx?state = MS
- www.seriousrunning.com/Trail-Running/Mississippi_35.html
- www.thebackpacker.com/trails/ms/

Trail Running

Missouri

- mostateparks.com/trails/lake-ozarks-state-park
- www.trails.com/findarea.aspx?state = MO
- www.traillink.com/stateactivity/mo-running-trails.aspx
- Cape Giradeau—www.visitcape.com/Hiking.aspx
- Kirksville—Thousand Hills Trail: 11 miles of woods, savannahs, streams, and wildlife.
- Blue Springs (east of Kansas City)—Landahl MTB trails: 20 miles of wonderful single track trails.
- Springfield—Several all-purpose paved trails.

Montana

- alltrails.com/us/montana/bozeman/trail-running
- www.trails.com/findarea.aspx?state = MT
- www.traillink.com/stateactivity/mt-running-trails.aspx
- Billings—Heading uphill from the university to the airport, stay to the left. Within a few hundred yards is a path that becomes a trail on a ledge with a beautiful view.
- Bozeman
- Cooke City, to East Rosebud—This 27-mile trail starts at 7,000 feet above sea level and rises to 10,000 feet along 7 lakes and 3 waterfalls.
- Livingston—Gallatin National Park: Ask about bears, however.
- Missoula—Check in with the Runner's Edge running store staff for trails. There's a great asphalt trail that goes along the river with many access points from downtown. www.missoulian.com/app/hikebike/
- Whitefish—www.allwhitefish.com/summer_recreation/hiking_backpacking.php

Nebraska

- www.trails.com/toptrails.aspx?state = NE
- www.trails.com/findarea.aspx?state = NE
- www.seriousrunning.com/Trail-Running/Nebraska_38.html
- www.traillink.com/stateactivity/ne-hiking-trails.aspx
- Lincoln—www.lincoln.ne.gov/city/parks/parksfacilities/trails; www.gptn.org/trails/info
- Omaha—www.localhikes.com/MSA/MSA_5920.asp

Nevada

- www.nvtrailmaps.com
- www.parks.nv.gov/trail
- www.trails.com/findarea.aspx?state = NV
- www.traillink.com/stateactivity/nv-hiking-trails.aspx
- www.seriousrunning.com/Trail-Running/Nevada_39.html
- www.nevadacitychamber.com/.../hiking-trails
- www.cityofhenderson.com/parks/parks/trails_and_bike
- Lake Tahoe, NV/CA—www.tahoerimtrail.org

New Hampshire

- www.nhstateparks.org/experience/hiking
- www.nhoutdoors.com/hiking_trails.htm
- www.trails.com/toptrails.aspx?state = NH
- www.seriousrunning.com/Trail-Running/New-Hampshire_40.html
- www.traillink.com/stateactivity/nh-hiking-trails.aspx
- Plache Wolfeboro to Sanbornville rail trail along Crescent and Wentworth lakes.

New Jersey

- www.njtrailrunning.com
- www.njhiking.com
- www.njtrails.org
- www.traillink.com/stateactivity/nj-running-trails.aspx
- www.trails.com/toptrails.aspx?state = NJ
- www.seriousrunning.com/Trail-Running/New-Jersey_41.html
- Spring Valley—Columbia Trail.
- Staten Island—Greenbelt trails: Great view on top of Moses Mountain.

New Mexico

- newmexico.sportsvite.com/sports/TrailRunning
- www.nmtrailrunning.blogspot.com
- www.seriousrunning.com/Trail-Running/New-Mexico_42.html
- www.traillink.com/stateactivity/nm-running-trails.aspx
- www.trails.com/findarea.aspx?state = NM

- Albuquerque—www.itsatrip.org/sports-outdoor/cycling-hiking.aspx
- Santa Fe—Dale Ball trails: Scenic single track trails that connect.

New York

- www.tripleblaze.com/Hiking-Trails/New-York_36.html
- www.canals.ny.gov/trails
- www.trails.com/toptrails.aspx?state = ny
- www.seriousrunning.com/Trail-Running/New-York_43.html
- www.traillink.com/stateactivity/ny-running-trails.aspx
- New York City—www.nycgovparks.org/parks/forestpark/facilities/hikingtrails
- www.slackpacker.com/map_ny.html
- www.ride-newyork.com/NYSTrailsCouncil.htm
- Staten Island—Greenbelt trails: Great view on top of Moses Mountain.

North Carolina

- www.rei.com/guidepost/list/north-carolina/hiking/nc/7
- www.traillink.com/stateactivity/nc-running-trails.aspx
- www.seriousrunning.com/Trail-Running/North-Carolina_44.html
- www.tripleblaze.com/Hiking-Trails/North-Carolina_37.html
- www.trailsofnc.com/index.html
- www.trails.com/toptrails.aspx?state = NC
- www.carolinaoutdoorsguide.com/HikingStateParks.html
- Research Triangle area near Raleigh—Olmstead Park: Lots of trails
- Durham—The Al Buehler Cross Country Trail in Duke Forest University trail is very challenging.

North Dakota

- www.parkrec.nd.gov/activities/hiking.html
- www.seriousrunning.com/Trail-Running/North-Dakota_45.html
- www.traillink.com/stateactivity/nd-running-trails.aspx
- northcountrytrail.org/trail/states/north-dakota/
- www.ndtourism.com/whatdo/activities/hiking

Ohio

- www.dnr.state.oh.us/facilitiesmaps/ohiohiking/tabid/502/
- www.traillink.com/stateactivity/oh-running-trails.aspx
- www.seriousrunning.com/Trail-Running/Ohio_46.html
- www.trails.com/findarea.aspx?state = OH
- Buckeye Trail—northcountrytrail.org/trail
- www.localhikes.com/MSA/MSA_1840.asp
- Burr Oak State Park

Oklahoma

- www.bestoklahomatrails.com
- www.seriousrunning.com/best/?c = 47
- www.trails.com/findarea.aspx?state = OK
- www.traillink.com/stateactivity/ok-running-trails.aspx
- Oklahoma City—www.okc.gov/trails
- www.oktrails.com

Oregon

- traveloregon.com/see-do/recreation/hiking/?utm_source = bing&utm_medium = cpc&utm_ term = Hiking&utm_campaign = Spring13
- www.trails.com/stateactivity.aspx?area = 14261
- www.seriousrunning.com/Trail-Running/Oregon_48.html
- www.traillink.com/stateactivity/or-hiking-trails.aspx
- Ashland—www.ashlandchamber.com/Page.asp?NavID = 914
- Eugene—Pre's Trail (See chapter 6.)
- Portland—Forest Park: Bbeautiful and goes for dozens of miles adjacent to downtown Portland. www.forestparkconservancy.org/portland-hiking-trails
- Beaverton—Geoff Hollister Trail near the Nike Campus (See chapter 6.)

Pennsylvania

- www.dcnr.state.pa.us/stateparks/recreation/hiking/index.htm
- www.trailsnet.com/Pennsylvania_trails.html
- www.trails.com/findarea.aspx?state = PA
- www.seriousrunning.com/Trail-Running/Pennsylvania_49.html

- Allentown area—Lehigh Valley trail.
- Philadelphia—A good trail system along the river in the downtown district.
- Pittsburgh—Lots of trails in the area, including several in the downtown district.

Rhode Island
- www.ritrails.com
- www.visitrhodeisland.com/what-to-do/hiking/
- www.trails.com/toptrails.aspx?state = RI
- www.traillink.com/trailsearch.aspx?state = RI
- www.seriousrunning.com/Trail-Running/Rhode-Island_50.html

South Carolina
- www.sctrails.net/trails
- www.southcarolinaparks.com/things-to-do/trails/hiking
- www.trails.com/toptrails.aspx?state = SC
- www.seriousrunning.com/Trail-Running/South-Carolina_51.html
- www.traillink.com/stateactivity/sc-walking-trails.aspx

South Dakota
- www.travelsd.com/Hiking
- www.traillink.com/stateactivity/sd-running-trails.aspx
- alltrails.com/us/south-dakota
- Deadwood—George Mickelson Trail: A beautiful, mostly non-paved rail trail through the Black Hills.

Tennessee
- www.tn.gov/environment/parks/findapark/hiking.shtml
- www.tennesseetrails.org
- alltrails.com/us/tennessee
- www.seriousrunning.com/Trail-Running/Tennessee_53.html
- www.trails.com/activity.aspx?area = 10894
- www.traillink.com/stateactivity/tn-running-trails.aspx
- Chattanooga—voices.yahoo.com/best-running-trails-chattanooga-tn-3702138.html

Texas

- www.Texastrails.org
- www.traillink.com/trailsearch.aspx?state = TX
- www.seriousrunning.com/Trail-Running/Texas_54.html
- www.trails.com/toptrails.aspx?area = 10021
- www.tpwd.state.tx.us/state-parks/parks/things-to-do/hiking-in-state-parks
- Houston Trail Runners Extreme—This has a list of Texas trails with information.
- Dallas and North Texas—www.nttr.org/html/trails.htm
- Grapevine Lake (near Dallas)—North shore trail from Rockledge Park.
- Tejas Trails—These go through the Guadalupe Mountains and are the venue for numerous trail races. www.tejastrails.com
- El Paso—Rio Grande River Levee Road from Borderland Road.

Utah

- www.utah.com/hike/
- www.traillink.com/traillist.aspx?state = UT&city = Salt + Lake...
- www.seriousrunning.com/Trail-Running/Utah_55.html
- Park City—Several scenic trails: www.parkcityhiking.com/winter-activities/trail-running
- Salt Lake City—www.utah.com/saltlake/hiking.htm
- Sandy—Jordan River trail (paved)
- Utah county—Timpanookee Trail: 7 miles to the summit for the mountain goat runners.

Vermont

- www.voga.org/Vermont_Recreation_Trails.htm
- www.trails.com/toptrails.aspx?state = VT
- www.traillink.com/state/vt-trails.aspx

Virginia

- www.traillink.com/stateactivity/va-running-trails.aspx
- www.seriousrunning.com/10/1069/Trail-Running/Fountainhead-Regional-Park.html
- Harper's Ferry—Appalachian trail: Varied terrain, great views.
- Charlottesville—www.charlottesville.org/Index.aspx?page = 1725
- Fairfax County—www.fairfaxcounty.gov/parks/trailsframe.htm

- Arlington/Crystal City/Alexandria—The Mt Vernon Trail goes along the Potomac River to Mt Vernon.
- Richmond—richmondgoodlife.com/richmond_trails.htm

Washington

- www.parks.wa.gov/trails
- www.runwashington.com/resources/running-trails.htm
- www.traillink.com/trailsearch.aspx?state = WA
- www.seriousrunning.com/10/2175/Trail-Running/Moran-State.
- http://www.trails.com/stateactivity.aspx?area = 14081
- Washington Trails Association www.wta.org/go-hiking/seasonal-hikes/.../state-park-hikes
- Bellingham—Interurban trail system, Fairhaven Park.
- Tacoma—Point Defiance
- Pullman—Moscow ID—Bill Chipman Palouse Trail. www.pullmancivictrust.org/Chipman.html
- Mt Saint Helens National Park—Hummocks Trail.
- Spokane—High Drive Bluffs.

West Virginia

- www.traillink.com/state/wv-trails.aspx
- www.trails.com/findarea.aspx?state = WV
- www.seriousrunning.com/Trail-Running/West-Virginia_59.html
- www.wvstateparks.com/parkmaps.html

Wisconsin

- www.trails.com/state-park-trails.aspx?keyword = state%20
- dnr.wi.gov/topic/parks/activities/hike.html
- www.traillink.com/stateactivity/wi-running-trails.aspx
- www.travelwisconsin.com
- www.anythingwisconsin.com/findatrail.htm
- Fish Creek and Door Country and Penninsula Park—Beautiful trails, with few uphills.
- Green Bay,—Baird Creek in the city of Green Bay.
- Stevens Point—A great trail near this city. greencircletrail.org

- Lake Geneva—22-mile trail around lake.
- Wisconsin's Dells—Trail around Devils Lake.www.devilslakewisconsin.com/activities/ hiking/

Wyoming
- www.seriousrunning.com/Trail-Running/Wyoming_61.html
- www.tripleblaze.com/Hiking-Trails/Wyoming_54.html
- alltrails.com/us/wyoming
- www.trails.com/findarea.aspx?state = WY
- www.traillink.com/stateactivity/wy-running-trails.aspx

Credits

Cover Design:	Sabine Groten
Cover photo:	© Thinkstock/Stockbyte
Layout and typesetting:	Kerstin Quadflieg
Copy editing:	Elizabeth Evans, Sebastian Meyer
Photos:	See individual photos